T0129395

WRONG TURNS, RIGHT MOVES
IN EDUCATION

Deborah Rhea, Ed.D.

ARCHWAY PUBLISHING

Archway Publishing books may be ordered through booksellers or by contacting:

Archway Publishing
1663 Liberty Drive
Bloomington, IN 47403
www.archwaypublishing.com
1 (888) 242-5904

Because of the dynamic nature of the Internet, any web addresses or
links contained in this book may have changed since publication and
may no longer be valid. The views expressed in this work are solely those
of the author and do not necessarily reflect the views of the publisher,
and the publisher hereby disclaims any responsibility for them.

This book is a work of non-fiction. Unless otherwise noted, the author
and the publisher make no explicit guarantees as to the accuracy of
the information contained in this book and in some cases, names of
people and places have been altered to protect their privacy.

Any people depicted in stock imagery provided by Getty Images are
models, and such images are being used for illustrative purposes only.
Certain stock imagery © Getty Images.

ISBN: 978-1-4808-7445-9 (sc)
ISBN: 978-1-4808-7446-6 (e)

Library of Congress Control Number: 2019901711

Print information available on the last page.

Archway Publishing rev. date: 03/22/2019

In Memory of Betty Dieb

FOREWORD

Sometimes you take a trip and discover something so amazing. Nutella crepes! Heated carpet! Vending machines that sell hard-boiled eggs! You can't understand why this great idea never made it to our shores or at least has yet to become ubiquitous. So it was when Debbie Rhea went to Finland and took a look at its schools.

In America, we think it is normal for five-year-olds—heck, three-year-olds—to be told to sit down and get to work. It's their job to learn not to squirm. We think it's fine to drill third graders in math problems, not so they understand how to double the amount of butter for a double batch of cookies but so they can pass a test that they, their teacher, and their school will be judged by.

We think nothing of canceling recess for the group of fifth-grade boys who were so desperately bored during reading time that they started horsing around. "No recess for them! They must stay inside and open their books." Movement becomes a crime; reading becomes punishment. This is what they are learning, and somehow we think that makes sense.

It does, if you think of school as prison. If we think students should arrive each day to obey with their heads down and don't upset the warden, they'll be rewarded with a bit of yard time. Of course some will tune out, others will act out. But what is the alternative?

That is what this book is about. The radical idea here is that there *is* an alternative and it's doable. When Debbie arrived in Finland, she found teachers who were given freedom to teach, students who were liberated from high-stakes tests, and abundant school time for kids to move, play, and think in a different way. Think with their bodies. Be creative. Organize a game. Start a project. Do something self-directed instead of simply following orders.

If Finland were at the bottom of the education world, it might make sense to ignore their ridiculously humane and optimistic example. But with all its recess, freedom, joy, and inclusiveness (as kids are not grouped by intellectual abilities), it is not at the bottom. It is at the top. It's almost as if treating kids like whole human beings is the way to get them to learn.

Debbie went on a journey and came back with new ideas that deserve to become ubiquitous. It is that journey she takes you on now.

Have a great trip.

Lenore Skenazy, president of Let Grow and founder of the Free-Range Kids movement

PREFACE

The United States always strives to be the best in the world at everything. This is not a bad quality to strive for, but over the past 30+ years, it seems the U.S. educational system has taken a wrong turn, focusing predominantly on standardized test scores to determine the success of our children to the detriment of a wholesome classroom environment conducive for learning. As the decision makers across the country continue to place more and more importance on a score, the physical, social, and emotional development of children has suffered.

Because of America's preoccupation to be the best, we have lost our way with what is right for kids. America's response to raise lower standardized test scores in all children has been to provide longer school days, increase minutes daily of content time, begin a child's school experiences as early as possible with more advanced curriculum, at times, than a child may be developmentally ready for, and restrict outdoor, unstructured play time.

Simply put, public schools across the country have not reached their full potential no matter how much money or resources are thrown at the system to improve the test score. Sadly this path is impeding our nation by producing some of the unhealthiest and stressed-out children we have ever seen.

During this same time period as a university professor, I was very much involved in studying children's motivational patterns to promote intrinsically driven children rather than using reinforcement-only tools that seemed to promote extrinsically driven children. I have been an educator for 39 years, but my role over the past 25+ years has been to prepare university students to be the next generation of quality physical education teachers in the K-12 setting while also being hired every summer to conduct in-service trainings for K-12 physical education teachers. I also published physical education curriculum for K-12 teachers to enhance their ability to guide children and adolescents to be more intrinsically motivated rather than have to be told what to do and then see students walk away and never engage in physical activity again.

Throughout my years working with teachers and students, I thought teachers were dropping the ball but subsequently began to realize that it wasn't the teachers as much as it was the classroom environment. My message for many years was that teachers needed to raise their expectations, teach with clear objectives daily, and recognize that their interactions with students wouldn't just impact those students but anyone those students came in contact with tenfold.

By 2011, I realized it didn't matter how high a teacher's expectations were or how quality the lesson was. The lack of focus and emotional stability—as well as the rise in childhood and adolescent chronic diseases—were creating a volatile classroom that prevented quality learning from taking place.

This environment has led to unstable teaching practices and, in many cases, less mentoring opportunities due on average to a five-year retention rate of teachers. Knowing that teachers become burned out in five years or less and students become burned out by third grade, I knew something had to be done. This book reflects my path as an educator for the past 39 years and why a six-week trip to Finland was necessary to remember why certain philosophies and principles should never be removed from schools.

ACKNOWLEDGMENTS

Thank you to the many individuals at Texas Christian University and the University of Helsinki who contributed to the opportunity and meaningfulness of my visit. Thanks also to the secretary of education for Finland; the spokesperson from the Finland Sports Federation; all of the principals, assistant principals, and teachers in the Finland comprehensive schools; and faculty from the University of Helsinki and University of Jyväskylä who allowed me to visit each of their campuses and classrooms. This was definitely a collaborative effort among all of the contributors. I also want to give a very special thank-you to the people who supported me hugely in this endeavor: my parents, the LiiNK team, and especially my best friend and collaborator, Carol.

INTRODUCTION

Life Lessons

My whole life has been about learning and reflecting on who I am as an educator and why I put myself out there every day to help children find their inner passion to be the best they can be in life. I feel I have been highly successful in my career and I am where I am today because I leave my options open, weigh the benefits of an opportunity based on my purpose and integrity, and make decisions based on intuition and analytics.

In order to understand my reflections about Finland, you need to first understand my journey. I have transitioned many times in my educational journey. Each transition or chapter has taken me to a higher understanding of our schools and lessons learned from previous experiences.

Life Chapter 1

I graduated with an undergraduate degree in exercise and sport studies with teacher certifications in physical education, health, and English. I spent my first 11 years in secondary schools teaching English and physical education and coaching volleyball, tennis, track, and cross-country. This spanned three different school districts: two high schools and one middle school. I learned so much from each school I taught and coached in. I especially learned how to teach in a confined space (the classroom) and an open space (the gymnasium and outdoors). They both had their advantages, and I developed strengths working in both arenas.

I realized in my tenth year as a teacher and coach that I didn't understand the psychology or motivation behind how kids made decisions anymore. They were changing. I decided to do something about this. I enrolled in a sport psychology class and loved it! I felt like I was beginning to understand my students a little better as I read the research, discussed issues in class, and worked with my students daily on these same principles learned in class. I began to understand as a coach and teacher why it is important to create scenarios where a child has the ability to make tough decisions and give him or her the opportunities to fail until he or she succeeds.

Lesson Learned

Not all kids will see your mentorship as you see it. Failure sometimes is the only way for some to learn.

Scenario of This Lesson

I was coaching cross-country and track. I was a runner myself and would run with the girls in the morning before school started. I decided to train for a marathon on my own time, although the girls knew I was planning for this event. They were training for a two-mile race so it never crossed my mind that what I was doing was having some influence on any of them.

It came time to run the marathon, and a few of the athletes had decided to run the half-marathon while I ran the marathon. I had told them it would be detrimental to their cross-country events to run a marathon and that they needed to only run the 10K or no more than the half-marathon if they were going to try this.

One of the girls didn't listen and ran the marathon, coming in behind me. I was furious. Why did she not listen? Why did she continue to complete that long race when she knew she hadn't trained to do it? Seeing her get injured, not be able to complete the season with her teammates, and never run cross-country competitively again made me reflect on the sport psychology course I was taking and why athletes make decisions sometimes that are detrimental to their success. Failure seemed to be the only option for learning a lesson. We can't always protect children from harm or hurt.

Life Chapter 2

The professor I had for the sport psychology class asked if I had thought about coming back to school to get a master's degree in sport psychology. I had not thought about it, but my professor was persuasive, and I must have been ready for a change. I knew I wouldn't be able to do my full-time teaching/coaching position and go to school. I knew others were able to do all of it at the same time, but not me.

I was ready to devote full time to school, so I asked my school district for a two-year sabbatical while I earned my master's degree. The school district granted that request, so I began going to school full time as a graduate assistant and teaching physical education courses at the university.

In my second year, I realized that I was even hungrier for understanding how people think, feel, and behave. This thought process took me to the next decision, to graduate with my master's degree and continue into my doctoral program at the same university with the same mentor. I completed both my master's and doctoral degrees in sport/exercise psychology and pedagogy. My primary line of research was studying gender and ethnicity body image and eating disorder issues in sport.

Lesson Learned

Make yourself as marketable as possible without overextending yourself. I didn't realize the positive impact these experiences would have in creating my niche in education until later in my career. This combination of emphasis areas with my research area made me very marketable at the university level with future faculty positions, training educators, and eventually working with school policies and procedures.

Life Chapter 3

Reality hit. I thought I would just stay in Houston and go to work consulting athletes on performance issues. There's not much money in doing this type of work unless you have a full-time job doing performance consulting as part of it. My mentor told me I had to leave Houston if I wanted to find a job at the university level. This is how I could do both: teach and consult athletes with performance issues. I said I would never go north of the Mason-Dixon Line.

Reality hit again. I was off to Iowa State University (ISU) to teach methods classes for physical education teachers and teach sport/exercise psychology classes.

Lessons Learned

Don't ever say never, and always keep an open mind. Opportunities are out there to be taken, but you have to listen and be ready when they appear.

Life Chapter 4

I absolutely loved Iowa State, but leadership changes led me to believe I needed to move on to a different location. Hence, I moved to Fort Worth to take a position as assistant professor in kinesiology at Texas Christian University. This was a great move, both personally and professionally. TCU has been very supportive of my research endeavors, my leadership abilities, and my vision/passion as an educator. I have been doing the same things at TCU that I began my university career doing at ISU. As life would have it, I have had a couple of other chapters develop while at TCU.

Life Chapter 5

As a full professor, the dean of my college wanted me to apply for the associate dean for research and health sciences position. That was not on my radar; nor was it something I thought I was prepared to do or was interested in doing. I was happy and content being a professor. I was a tenured, successful researcher as well as successful educator. I was writing physical education curriculum for school districts and doing in-service trainings for K-12 schools. Life was good. No new chapters were needed … or so I thought.

Well, the opportunity arose. I listened. I thought about my strengths and the possibilities that this position held and decided to take the position. As with every other decision I have made and chapters that have evolved, I didn't plan my life out to have certain things by certain times. My life has truly been a journey of opportunities that have helped me grow and be better than I was before the next challenge appeared. Ten years later, I am still in this position.

1. If you take on more, you have to give something up. You only have so much time in your day. In order to stay healthy and happy, professional and personal life have to remain balanced. Balance is essential.
2. Focus on your strengths; use those strengths to build your wheelhouse. If you only think about your weaknesses, you will never accomplish what you set out to do. They will hold you back.

Lesson Chapter 6

Again, I was not looking for another change in my life. I was happy and content preparing physical education teachers, mentoring/supporting faculty with research endeavors, and handling student issues. But the cards were obviously saying something different. My neighbor brought a *Smithsonian* magazine[1] over in August 2011. She said there was an article in there that reminded her of who I was and suggested I might be interested in reading it.

I remember looking at her and thinking how nice of her to think about me. What I didn't realize is the article provided a new opportunity and piqued my interest hugely. The title of the article was "From F to A+: How Finland Changed Their Educational System for the Better."[1]

My passion for preparing the best physical education teachers to handle the challenges in schools today took me to Finland to learn more about what they were doing that created such a productive learning environment for 30+ years.

Several things had to happen for this trip to take place. I had to ask for and receive a semester-long leave with pay from my university (TCU) to travel to Finland. I had to set up a host site with a university in Finland; confirm a faculty member who would work with me on all types of connections I would need in the schools, the universities, and the Finnish Board of Education; as well as consider research possibilities.

I had to find a place to live once I knew which university would be hosting me. I also wanted to make some connections with school districts about my upcoming visit. During that preparation year of waiting to depart for Finland, quite a few magazine articles, books, and documentaries highlighting Finland's educational system and culture were published. [2,3,4,5] I read and listened to as much as I could about where I was going and what to expect. Through my readings, the following evidence-based research, "Crossroads for the U.S.," set the stage for my educational experiences in Finland.

Crossroads for the U.S.

A disconcerting shift toward increased classroom time at the expense of physical education and recess has created a detrimental effect on children. [1, 2, 3] The results of the belief that increased classroom content time will ultimately produce better learners have been lackluster at best. [4, 5] While the importance of classroom time for students is indisputable, it must be recognized that time spent daily in an increased number of specific content minutes is only as valuable as the quality of delivery and the willingness of children to receive the information. [6] The opportunity to play and be physically active leads to better mental acuity and socialization skills, but both have been minimized within the school day for increased classroom time and safety issues. [4, 7] When schools confine students to the indoors with limited time to play and socialize for much of the seven-plus hours they are in school, their brains become less receptive, and many negative behaviors occur, such as bullying and aggression. [8, 9]

THE BEGINNING: FINNISH EDUCATION REFLECTIONS

All eyes are on Finland, as it seems to be ahead of the curve with its forward thinking and educational model. The United States could learn from Finland's perspective on education. It's not that the United States doesn't want the best education for children, but the path taken over the past thirty years has lost sight of crucial developmental elements necessary for healthier, happier, more well-adjusted children, trading these in for test scores.

The purpose of my visit to Finland was to observe the Finnish children in their K-12 school environment, take in the concepts and teaching strategies of the teachers in the K-12 school setting, and develop a model for integrating some of these successful concepts into a pilot program that hopefully would start in the Dallas–Fort Worth metroplex. My research schedule was designed around six weeks of weekdays only. Weekends were designed for exploration of the Finnish culture. This equated to a series of reflections about how people live in Finland, how Finland tackles education, and how the United States could learn from the Finnish educational model. The six-week research schedule, coordinated by one of my three sponsors (named Faculty 1), can be found in appendix A. This was an arduous task, and I am very grateful for all of the time and energy she gave to make sure I was able to be as successful as I was learning all about the different facets of Finnish education.

REFLECTION 1

LANDED IN HELSINKI

I flew into Helsinki with very good feelings but also a little trepidation and fear. I didn't know the Finnish language; nor did I know the layout of the city. I settled into the apartment I rented for six weeks and ventured out to a grocery store. My first challenge was reading labels on food items. I couldn't tell butter from yogurt. I then tried to pick an orange juice. I could tell from the carton picture that it was orange juice, but I couldn't tell if it had pulp or not. I finally went to check out, where I realized that I didn't have a bag with me to carry the items I purchased. I didn't realize at the time that I could purchase one from the store. So off I went with eight items in my arms. Thank goodness I only lived about a block from the market. I felt very much like a fish out of water, but I survived the day. I wrote my three sponsors from the University of Helsinki and set appointments to meet in person.

REFLECTION 2

—————————————————————————▶

HOST MEETINGS AND INTRODUCTION OF SCHEDULE

What a difference a day makes! I woke up worried about finding my way to the university since all of the streets had very long names that were very hard to pronounce. One of the faculty gave me some brief directions, which I then used to try to locate the university on a map of Helsinki before setting out that morning. I couldn't find two of the streets on the map, so I decided I would figure it out as I went. Once I started walking, I realized that it wasn't going to be bad at all. It took me about thirty minutes to find the university and the building where I was to meet my new colleagues. After meeting them, I realized this was going to be a great trip with great new friends to help me along the way.

One of my first tasks was to speak with one of the pedagogy classes, a group of about eighteen. Great students! They all spoke English. I loved meeting them. I would be seeing these students throughout the six weeks of my stay in Helsinki. We would get to know each other better as time went on.

After spending a few hours at the university, I was able to get around Helsinki and still make it back to my apartment without incident. I am directionally challenged, so it was awesome to know that I could maneuver and still get back to home base. I was able to see a couple of things while out and about. One of my favorite places—which ended up being my go-to place every day—was the Lutheran church in the square. This church has a magnificent presence in Helsinki, with two massive levels of steps for sitting or using to enter the church. I loved sitting there daily to put my thoughts together, watch the people milling about in the square, and observe the ships entering the harbor. One of the best phrases I learned in the first week was *moi moi*. Saying *moi* twice means "goodbye," whereas saying it once means "hi."

REFLECTION 3

THE FINNISH STUDENT AND PUPIL– FITNESS AND ASSESSMENT DEBATE

This week was focused on learning more about how a Finnish university prepares physical education and classroom teachers. The first day of this week took me to the University of Helsinki to observe Faculty 2. He had a class of about eighteen students (two men and sixteen women) studying to be classroom teachers with a minor in physical education.

The first class I observed was focused on assessment, meaning they were learning how to assess pupils in physical education. The professor focused the lesson on fitness and asked them to debate why fitness testing should or shouldn't be used in primary and secondary schools.

As a side note, the Finnish people refer to university students as students and children in the K-12 schools as pupils. So from this point forward, I will refer to them using those terms.

Finnish students, in general, do not seem to like fitness testing. It seems most of the students would have preferred to debate why fitness testing should not be used in the schools, but they had to be on one side or the other.

To give a point of reference, the university and public schools in Finland have adopted the Fitnessgram tests,[1] which are used today in many American schools. These tests are popular in America because they are criterion-referenced (minimum standards for fitness termed "healthy fitness zones" [HFZ]) instead of norm-referenced standards (comparing one to all others). The Cooper twelve-minute run test, curl-ups, and push-ups are used in grades five and up in Finland.

As the students debated why they did or didn't want fitness testing in the schools, it became evident that American students and pupils are very similar in many ways to them. The pupils have problems with bullying in Finland, just as in the United States. When they execute the Cooper twelve-minute run test, bullying can arise because of the teacher delivery of the test outcomes. The teachers seem to record the test scores but don't explain that, if the students receive above a certain score, they are considered to be in the HFZ, which means they are healthy and fit on cardiovascular endurance. Each test also records the HFZ by gender and age. Therefore, if the healthy fitness zone for grade-five boys on the cardiovascular PACER test was twenty-three to sixty-one laps (twenty meters per lap),[1] then the teacher should explain, if the students reach that range, they are considered healthy for cardiovascular endurance. If they do not reach the lower number of the range, then they should be told they are in the "needs improvement zone" (NI). The teachers don't seem to help the pupils get any better if they are NI. Therefore, the pupils who are good at running make fun of the pupils who don't do as well on the test. The pupils who are at the top of their class will just get better, and the pupils who come in lower lose confidence for the next time the test is executed. This creates a negative feeling in some of the pupils, so they don't want to participate in class activities presently or as they get older.

The students also discussed time constraints. Formal physical education is only offered twice a week for about forty-five minutes each time in the older grades. The Finnish students felt that twice a week is not enough to prepare the pupils for successful cardio testing. The teachers also don't require much running in the physical education classes because they want to make it fun for the pupils. Both of these reasons are similar to what happens in the United States. These two reasons complicate testing cardiovascular endurance in Finland and contribute to why, overall, the students don't want fitness testing in the schools.

I have my students debate this same question at TCU in both elementary and secondary methods classes. Is there a need to evaluate or assess a pupil for fitness with standardized scores? My primary reason for visiting Finland was to observe how their system functions without standardized tests. I could tell from the students' discussion that they don't want a standardized method of evaluation in Finland schools. They feel that pupils should understand how an assessment facilitates learning of skills, not what a score means.

The second class I observed that day was a track and field lab. Students went to a track very close to the Helsinki Olympic Park. It was a great place to practice skills and learn from each other. Before they began their own learning of skills, they were able to observe the elementary-aged children participate in a track meet. The pupils competed in two required events (60-meter run and throwing).

They had a choice of one other event: long jump or high jump. Most of them picked long jump. The way the events were set up created more standing around and less action than I would have wanted to see with elementary pupils in the United States. Interestingly, American pupils would have misbehaved and caused more discipline issues if given the opportunity to stand around, whereas the Finnish pupils did not misbehave or get off task at all.

After observing the pupils, the university students went outside the track area to a grassy throwing field. They taught javelin and discus to each other. Children learn javelin skills from age eight and up. They use a plastic javelin (very short) to introduce the skill to the younger children. Then they advance to a rubber javelin and then on to the actual javelin when the pupils are old enough. It was really interesting to watch the methods of this skill.

REFLECTION 4

---------------→

UNIVERSITY OF HELSINKI

One of my first goals in the second week was to purchase a travel card for transportation in and around Helsinki. Walking to different places within the city is not hard at all, but getting from one end of the city to the other can be at least four to five miles. So having a travel card helps when moving from one school to the next on a time schedule. Up to this point, walking was the best way to see everything and understand my surroundings. Helsinki is very accessible overall though. The rest of the observations in this second week were going to be located an hour outside of Helsinki. There are different options for the type of card to have and how much it costs in order to travel around Helsinki proper or to go somewhere outside of Helsinki.

So on this day, I walked in a new direction to find the train station where cards could be purchased. Once purchasing a card, loading the card with additional funds can be done anywhere in town. I then went on an hour-long walk to explore other areas of Helsinki. I saw children playing soccer in a park, lots of people riding bikes or walking to work/school, and several people eating at outdoor bakeries. It's a great culture for physical activity and especially being outdoors. My brain began to recognize the stark contrast between the Finns and Americans. Being outdoors was a way of life for the Finns, whereas Americans have moved indoors over the past thirty years for just about everything.

After exploring, I walked to the university to meet Faculty 2 again for a class examining Polar accelerometers, which measure how much time children are active versus how much time they are sedentary. I was given an accelerometer to wear for the rest of the week/weekend. The students were measuring active time of pupils for a five-day period. This meant that the pupils would wear the accelerometers even when bathing, sleeping, or swimming.

I tried the Korean eatery for lunch. Good food! Then I met with one more university class working on outdoor education concepts for kindergarten pupils. This is a new concept for me to work with children this young on outdoor education skills. In reality, they were emphasizing creativity even though they called it outdoor education. Their goal was to decide which collaborative tasks they could introduce to young children in an early childhood setting. This meant they would engage pupils in different sensory tasks in the forest through orienteering skills. Each group of university students I observed would work on the sensory tasks and try them on each other before trying them on the kindergarten pupils. I observed their interactions with the pupils and discuss in a future reflection.

By the middle of the second week, I began to feel emotional fatigue. I think this was because of the language disparity and the amount of information I was consuming daily. For a couple of days, I had to rest in the afternoons to recharge emotionally. My thought at this time was I hoped I would catch up on my sleep, relax my brain from being in learning mode for eight hours at a time, and be ready to go again to start the next week.

Speaking the language is very difficult, but I noticed understanding some of the words they spoke was easier. The more I immersed myself in their language, the better I became at recognizing words and understanding what they meant. The faculty were so good though to translate the classes for me or, at times, speak in English so I could understand the interactions.

REFLECTION 5

THE FINNISH LIFESTYLE

The following are facts I had learned by the end of the second week:

1. They have walking/biking trails that connect every part of the city and islands to each other.
2. They laugh a lot.
3. They believe in physical activity as a way of life.
4. They say fast-food places are becoming more evident and are concerned about it.
5. They believe saunas should be used daily, and most houses have one, like pools in the United States.
6. They believe in the health of their children and teach from a health perspective.
7. Teachers are required to have a master's degree to be hired as a teacher. The trend is to hire teachers with a PhD over master's level, if given the opportunity.

Some thoughts about the above facts in the following two sections.

Physical Activity Patterns

The Finns seem to be much more active than Americans are. They don't believe so. They feel that they have declined a lot. This is interesting since I only have a snapshot of who they are. My point of reference tells me something different than what they have seen over the past few years.

The Finns believe all individuals across the life span should get more than two hours of physical activity daily. The Center for Disease Control and Prevention (CDC) and United States Department of Health and Human Services (USDHHS) guidelines state younger children through preadolescence should accumulate at least sixty minutes of daily physical activity, whereas, adolescence and adult populations should get at least thirty minutes of physical activity daily.[1, 2] The Finns definitely stress more active minutes throughout the day, focusing on an active lifestyle for all ages, than Americans. They believe, even though people may get exercise in the evenings after they get off work for an hour or two, it's not enough to offset all of the sitting they do during the day.

I was blown away with that knowledge. The CDC[1] states that, if we get thirty minutes or more daily of moderate physical activity, we will be healthy. The Finns believe that is not enough at all and especially with all of the sitting that takes place throughout the day. What stands out most about the Finns is they believe in a holistic way of living from active time to using a sauna to work/leisure balance to outdoor exposure daily, which leads their population to be very happy with who they are and the lives they lead.

According to the World Health Organization (WHO),[3] physical inactivity has been identified as the fourth-leading risk factor for global mortality, causing an estimated 3.2 million deaths globally. Lifestyle habits need to be adjusted in the United States if our children are going to have a chance at a long, healthy life.

Teacher Education Standards

Finnish universities are designed so a bachelor's degree in education is earned in three years or less. Then the Finnish students are required to earn their master's degree in education, which takes two more years in order to teach. This is no different than a 3-2 or 4-1 teacher certification program in the United States. The difference though is that Finnish teachers are required to have the master's degree before they can teach at all. Teachers are very well respected in Finland. They put a lot of value on the amount of work it takes to become a teacher, and they respect the differences in the ways teachers teach.

I think we do a great job in many of our American universities preparing teachers as undergraduates. It takes four to five years to become a teacher in the United States if they go the traditional teacher certification route. I think this is still the best method of educating our teachers.

Where I think we go wrong is with alternative certifications. This is a method that became an option at least twenty years ago when the school climate began to deteriorate and discipline options became limited. This led to experienced and effective teachers leaving the field. State education agencies realized many teaching fields were hard to fill so they designed alternative programs to hire professionals in the field to take a few short courses and begin teaching in their respective professional subject, such as science, math, and languages. They felt this was the only way to recruit teachers for vacant positions in a short time span to fill needed positions each year.

This way of thinking has led to a preconceived idea that it is easy to become an educator/teacher. The Finnish culture understands and values what it takes to be a quality teacher as well as the influence teachers have on pupils and students graduating and becoming the next generation in their workforce. I hope the United

States begins to understand that being a teacher is one of the most important roles a person can train to do. When proper teaching methodology is missing, hired individuals in those positions will quit after a short period of time.

REFLECTION 6

ORIENTEERING/OUTDOOR EDUCATION IN FINLAND

Orienteering is a huge activity in Finland. The basic idea in orienteering is to proceed on a designated course from start to finish by visiting a number of control points in a predetermined order with the help of a map and/or compass. Finnish people have devised maps for all types of locations from school areas to parks to cross-country landscapes. Kindergarten through twelfth-grade schools in the United States have not created maps for their landscapes like the Finns, which is something I would like to see happen. Pupils in Finland begin orienteering around the age of ten and continue learning different techniques through the middle-school years.

Although the younger pupils do not do orienteering, they do participate in maps and sensory play. I travelled out to a park/lake where Faculty 1 and her university students met to set up orienteering activities around the park. They taught each other how to do the different elements on the course and spent time reading the different maps and finding the targets at each of the landmarked areas from the map. It was a lot of fun to watch them learn and problem solve the instructions they might give. They learned the way they gave instructions did not necessarily mean the same thing to the others listening to the instructions. This was a great learning experience for them and me.

After going through each of the four courses designed and set up, the students made a campfire for us to roast sausages and eat lunch. We then did one more map-reading activity to find a series of targets before departing midafternoon for Helsinki. This experience was about watching the faculty interact with their students to introduce a variety of physical activities. They teach very similarly to the U.S. methods programs, but they have taught orienteering in elementary schools for many years now and use this as a way to learn responsibility, social skills, and problem-solving skills early in the child's life.

REFLECTION 7

HIGH RESPECT FOR TEACHERS IN FINLAND

It is a well-known fact that teachers and professors are very highly respected in Finland. As mentioned in an earlier reflection, all teachers must have earned a master's degree before they can enter the classroom or the gymnasium to teach. At the elementary level, the classroom teacher is prepared to teach Finnish, science, math, social studies, and one of the following three areas: physical education, music, or art.

For someone to teach only physical education, he or she must earn the physical education master's degree. Then he or she meets the requirements to teach the lower (grades seven through nine) or upper (three years of high school) secondary school setting students. Only one university in Finland educates students to be physical education teachers with the master's degree needed, Jyväskyla University. It is located about three hours north of Helsinki by train and has a population of about 131,000. Only 80 physical educators are trained at this university at a time in the master's program, and all of them will be hired at a Finnish school when they graduate. Each of the universities is highly selective with the students for each discipline, so these physical education students are the cream of the crop. There is a need for more physical educators, but they don't have the resources to train more than 80 per group at this university.

This is such a different situation than in the United States. We have plenty of university graduates in physical education and very few jobs for them. U.S. secondary physical education-specialized students should be able to teach a second content area in order to be hired most of the time as a teacher.

One degree of separation between Finland and the United States is the teacher-coach relationship. In the United States, coaching is valued and respected as highly in preadolescent and adolescent schools as content teaching is in the same age groups in Finland. Many U.S. college students who want to major in secondary physical education have a primary goal to be hired as a coach. In many states hiring high school teachers, only head coaches are awarded the physical education teaching jobs. This leaves many pre-service physical educators who are more motivated to teach physical education rather than coach without jobs.

Hiring physical educators as coaches first can lead to a lack of respect in the physical education profession in the United States. Many coaches who have been hired as physical education teachers put more time and energy into working with the students who have an interest in playing a sport rather than the time and energy necessary to improve the activity and skill levels of the most vulnerable children in their classes.

On the other hand, Finnish schools don't hire physical educators for the elementary positions. They must be classroom teachers who also teach physical education. So the Finnish universities already steer their students into the classroom instead of training them to be physical educators with the result being too few jobs or none at all. They are essentially controlling supply and demand through what they offer and where.

I wish Finnish schools hired certified physical educators in the elementary schools, but I also wish the United States would hire physical educators who did not coach in the secondary schools. The bottom line is that physical education as a content is highly respected in Finland, whereas physical education as a content is not as highly respected in the United States. The way educators view the purpose and strengths that physical education brings to children and adolescents has to improve.

As long as U.S. schools continue to believe physical education is not a necessity, the further away children will move from a healthy mind-set and body. The overweight and obesity rates continue to be too high in the United States, especially in young children. Physical education—along with many other specials like music, art, crafts, and unstructured play—can be avenues to generate and stimulate cognition, physical capabilities, socialization, and emotional stability.

REFLECTION 8

PHYSICAL EDUCATION UNIVERSITY CLASSES

I observed two university physical education methods classes on this day. Each class was conducted in the Finnish language, but I seemed to understand quite a bit just by watching them interact. The professors would interpret major questions or issues so I would know what the topics were. The first class was a sociology of sport class. One of the activities the professor asked the students to engage in had to do with statements related to physical education issues.

The students were split into groups of three or four and then asked to discuss each of the statements, one at a time. It was really interesting to see how the students felt about certain issues and why. Sometimes their experiences with physical education personally drove some of their answers, but most of the time they really thought about the statement and why they felt the way they did on the topic.

One of the statements was, "PE as a school subject always reflects the values of the time."

Another was, "It is clear that PE has to serve competitive sports."

There were 10 total. These are statements that professors in the United States ask of their methods students as well, but the way they structured their thoughts and discussion was very good. These types of activities generate true respect for one another that, in turn, foster respect for Finnish physical education teachers in the profession.

The other class I observed was a physical education methods course. I had heard about Finland's version of baseball and was able to observe the physical education students from the University of Helsinki learn how to teach it. I have played different forms of baseball before like Danish baseball, but I wasn't sure whether the Finns played the game as the Danes or differently.

Well, I definitely experienced Finnish baseball and loved their version of the game. It is definitely different from Danish or American baseball. It's set up with three bases to run around, but they are set up 15 or so meters away from home base where the game begins. Also the pitcher stands on the opposite side of the home base from the batter and tosses the ball in the air for the batter to hit.

A picture of the setup can be seen on the next page. The surface of the field I observed was gravel. They drew lines on the surface with a tree branch or stick. The bases were drawn out the same way. I found it interesting that the playing surface was usually gravel. In the United States, we would consider all the injuries that could happen on such a surface and decide not to have the activity rather than provide instruction when it comes to how to avoid injury and so on. It's just a thought. Quite a few surfaces were like this in parks and on school grounds.

The only physical base is home, which is round and positioned between the batter and the pitcher. The batter's job is to step into the swing and strike the ball as the pitcher tosses it over the base. The other bases are drawn into the gravel with a stick. First base is actually down the left line, as labelled in the diagram. Second base is down the right line behind the pitcher's right foot, and third base is back behind first base and to the left just a little bit more.

No one is ever tagged out. An out only occurs when the ball is caught on the base by a teammate before the runner gets to the base. It's a great game and a lot of fun to watch or play. It definitely allows for more student participation and less standing and watching one or two people engage in the game.

Baseball, Nordic Style
A look at Pesäpallo, the Finnish version of the game

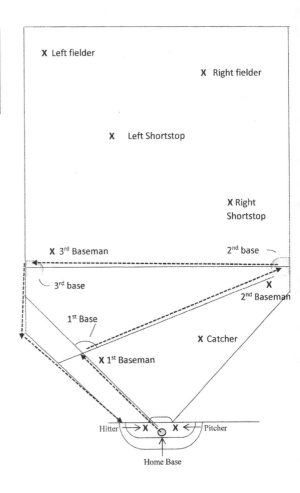

Baseball Nordic Style

REFLECTION 9

PERINTEISSÄ (TRADITION), PERHEISSÄ (FAMILY), SIVISTYS (CULTURE OR EDUCATION)

The Finnish vocabulary is so interesting, but better yet are some of the terms I learned in the short period of time I was in Finland. These terms are very reflective of the Finns and are taught across the generations. I was able to talk with a number of people from different aspects of education and the community in the first two weeks. These three terms are a good way to discuss some similarities and differences between the United States and Finland. When I first arrived, I thought I would see so many differences and very few similarities. That has not been the case.

Perinteissä (tradition) is very important in Finland. Some of their traditions are very similar to Americans: Christmas (*Joulu*), St. Valentine's Day (*Ystävän Päivä*), and Easter (*Pääsiäinen*). Of course my favorite common tradition is Christmas. Lapland, Finland, is the official site of the North Pole.[1] This is the northernmost region of Finland on the Arctic Circle, while Helsinki is the southernmost region of Finland.

I've been told the normal temperature there is -4 degrees Fahrenheit. This is the site of the official Santa post office.[2] Visitors from all parts of the world come to see Santa, the reindeer, Santa's workshop, and the official post office. While there, they can stay in an ice hotel, drink out of ice glasses, and sit on ice chairs.

The Finns are not known for as many food traditions, but they do have some that I would recommend. The first that I tried and liked was a rice pie called *Karjalanpiirakka*. It's a rice porridge stuffed in a rye crust. It is best served with *munavoi*, a mixture of hard-boiled eggs and butter. Another favorite is a pastry called *Korvapuusti* (cinnamon and cardamom buns). I'm not a fish eater, but they make many good fish dishes from soups to casseroles.

The Finnish culture is full of traditions, but some can be very different depending on the region that you are talking about.

Perheissä (family) is an important social concept in Finland and the United States. In both countries, if a child has both parents, on average, they both work. Both countries have an assorted mix of what a family looks like and how a family is defined. The family is still the cornerstone for the upbringing of children, and when the family unit is intact and healthy, the children seem to thrive. When the family unit is unhealthy, the child seems to be compromised and struggles to find success in life.

It doesn't matter what country one lives in. The family is important, and interaction among family members is key. I've talked with middle school-aged pupils in Finland who tell me they work so they can help with their family income. Similar situations happen in the United States as well.

Some readers might think all Finnish families are healthier and settled, but that's not the case. The percentage of family units struggling are probably much less, but they still have problems there, just like the United States.

Sivistys (culture/education) is a topic I will spend more time on in future entries. This is where there seem to be many differences. Here are some stats on Finland's culture.[3]

- **Location:** Northern Europe, Scandinavia, bordering Norway 729 kilometers, Sweden 586 kilometers, Russia 1,313 kilometers
- **Capital:** Helsinki
- **Climate:** cold temperate; potentially subarctic but comparatively mild because of moderating influence of the North Atlantic Current, Baltic Sea, and more than 60,000 lakes
- **Population:** 5.5 million (2018 est.)[4]
- **Ethnic Makeup:** Finn 93%, Swede 6%, Sami 0.11%, Roma 0.12%, and Tatar 0.02%
- **Religions:** Evangelical Lutheran 89%, Russian Orthodox 1%, none 9%, and other 1%
- **Government:** Republic

Fancy a Sauna?

The sauna has a special role in the domestic life of Finns. It is an experience shared with family and friends. Important business meetings may be followed by a sauna in which the conversation is continued on a more informal basis.

Saunas are found everywhere: At the end of calendar year 2017, there were 1.2 million saunas in private apartments and another 800,000 in summer cottages and public swimming pools. This translates to more than 3 million saunas for a population of 5.5 million.[5]

By reading the above stats, one might sense there is not much diversity in Finland. That can be deceiving though. In the past five to six years, there has been an 8 to 10 percent increase of individuals moving in from other countries.[6] The changes over the past few years have not changed the quality of the Finnish culture or educational system. The Finnish people understand how to create and sustain equality. They are much more cooperative than competitive in their lifestyle. They are a very responsible people in manners, clean environment, and acceptance. Equality, cooperation, and being responsible are key areas I focused on and really strived to understand before leaving their country.

Many differences exist in the United States by comparison. We are very diverse with many languages spoken, but there aren't many individuals who speak multiple languages. We have many religions and cultures among us, and we are a much larger population.

With that being said, there is still much we can learn from the Finns. One key difference—and one that I think we need to do a better job of—is learning different languages. Any student attending a Finnish school is required to study the native language (as a content area) every year from the time he or she enters the school at grade one (age seven) until he or she exits high school. Students are also required to learn at least one other language minimally, usually English. Many of the students will also learn Swedish as part of the curriculum throughout their years. They do not begin learning a second language until third grade.

Many schools in the United States have moved to dual-language programs, thinking this is a better way of teaching children from different languages. It was interesting to see the very different way of integrating pupils into the Finnish schools and how successful the pupils seem to be with immersion of the Finnish language.

The third week of observations was focused on visiting some of the elementary schools and learning about the ways they teach, how they integrate curriculum into such a short time period each week, and how they work with the pupils.

REFLECTION 10

A FINNISH ELEMENTARY SCHOOL DAY

In Finland, the school day looks very different from a school day in the United States. In Finland, grades one and two go to school approximately four and a half hours per day (8:00 a.m. to 12:30 p.m. or 9:00 a.m. to 1:30 p.m.), whereas for grades three through six, they will go to school approximately five and a half hours daily.

Over a five-day period of time, the schools are required to focus on a number of content areas. For example, they will learn Finnish just like we would learn English. They will also learn math, physical education, environmental studies (science related), religion or ethics, music, art, and crafts. Each of the content areas listed has a designated number of hours they must minimally meet each week.

Appendix B has a chart that reflects the number of hours per week the teachers must cover the different contents required for grades one through nine. So in a five-day week and only meeting four and a half to five and a half hours a day, this equates to a total of 22.5 to 27.5 hours a week of total time in school. To meet the required hours for the content areas, they will spend 15 to 19 hours of the above total hours a week in the classroom. This is because the country mandates recess be provided for 15 minutes each hour of the school day. So traditionally, it would look like diagram 1 below. Recess for the elementary-aged pupils usually reflects unstructured, outdoor play. The teachers will take them outside to run and play most of the time. Only when the temperature outside is extremely cold (subzero) will they play indoors.

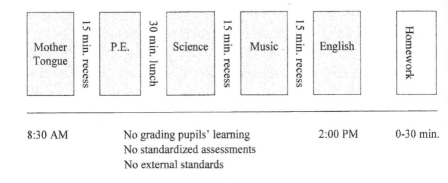

| Mother Tongue | 15 min. recess | P.E. | 30 min. lunch | Science | 15 min. recess | Music | 15 min. recess | English | Homework |

8:30 AM	No grading pupils' learning		2:00 PM	0-30 min.
	No standardized assessments			
	No external standards			

Sample Finland Daily Grade 3 Schedule

The teacher at the elementary level is trained to teach all 13 content areas. When it comes to his or her knowledge of art, music, physical education, or crafts, each teacher has an emphasis that he or she takes while getting his or her degree. For some, it would be art; for others, it would be music. Quite a few of the teachers have physical education backgrounds. What that means is, when it's time for those content areas, teachers who have more knowledge in each of those areas might teach to those areas and swap pupils for those disciplines.

Since each teacher has command of the content and the schedule, each one can decide which content areas will be taught each day and for how long to meet the total hours per week required since the teacher teaches all of the content.

Elementary school includes grades one through six. So for the third through sixth grades, they also have specific hours required for the different content areas. The teacher still has command of the schedule, just like for grades one and two. One difference at these age levels is that the school day is longer, about five and a half hours. The other difference is that they add history around fourth grade and a foreign language by third grade.

The languages are a big deal for the Finnish. They learn Finnish only in the early grades. Then in third grade, they usually begin to learn English. Then in the next couple of years, they add a third language, usually Swedish. I talked to several children who had learned up to four languages by seventh grade and were going to be learning a fifth language before high school. Usually the fourth language is German and the fifth language is French.

Are the U.S. students behind the game here? If we were keeping score, the Finnish would be way ahead of us on this one. They switch languages like ball caps. It's nothing for them to speak Finnish and then turn to me and talk in English. They love to speak English because they don't get to use their skills as often as they do in Finnish and Swedish.

Another facet of their required curriculum that I think impacts the overall development of the child in a big way is the dedicated time to religion or ethics for each grade level. They have several religions in Finland, but their primary religion is Lutheran. Until a couple of years ago, the country stated that, if a school had two or more pupils who practiced a particular religion, those pupils would be taught that religion each week. If the schools didn't have anyone who could teach religion to each representative group, then they had a person from that religion come teach the pupils. If the pupil did not have a religion (atheist or agnostic) or there was only one student representing a religion, those students took ethics.

Much discussion has been had about the growth in the number of different religions and the added expense that it has had on the schools. No decision has been made yet on whether to continue teaching religion in the schools or to change to an ethics course only, but they did change the way they presented the message. The schools now state that, if the parents want their pupils taking a specific religion, they will provide it with the same rules above, but if they don't prefer the religion, then the pupil will take ethics. This seems to have cut down quite a bit on how many different religions are taught in the schools.

In the United States, social-emotional learning (SEL) is gaining some traction as a topic to address in schools. The debate is whether to focus on a philosophy of good character across the school or to embed a character curriculum into the school day when SEL is considered. From my perspective, this is a huge piece that is missing from many schools and could make a huge difference in how children behave in and outside of the schools. All children need to feel safe, respect others and themselves, be trustworthy and honest, and think before they act. Introducing a character curriculum into schools could help to change the learning environment. The middle school and high school structures are reflected later in the book.

REFLECTION 11

THE K-12 SCHOOLS SHOULD NOT EQUATE TO DAYCARE

Educational decision makers in the United States need to have some thoughtful and respectful dialog about the purpose of the K-12 school system. I feel it is only right to put the unspoken truth out there for a topic that I believe needs change and a pendulum shift. One of the main reasons I came to Helsinki was to identify quality, not quantity, ways to educate our children and then send them home or elsewhere for play and creative time. (And I mean that. Get away from the computers and video games that have stifled children's ability to socialize, problem solve, and be healthy.)

When I was a young child (40+ years ago), children walked to school (not necessarily uphill in the snow), a parent or guardian for the majority of children was at home when the children arrived, and children played outside most of the afternoon until time for dinner (supper). The family ate together, and homework was completed with some supervision to make sure it was completed. Children slept at least eight hours each night and ate three home-cooked meals daily. Children were expected to do their work in school and homework after school. If they misbehaved or were disrespectful at school, the parents punished the child first and then asked what happened. There was order in the classroom, and children were active in physical education classes and unstructured play at least two hours each day.

Much has changed in the United States over the past few years: the family unit; expectations of school administrators, teachers, and community; the location where learning takes place; respect for authority and each other (general moral and ethical behaviors); and in many instances, the absent parent in the whole process. It used to be that one parent would go to work and the other parent would stay home and raise the children. Today, most parents/ guardians work in order to feed, clothe, and put a roof over their family's heads.

Usually parents or guardians work past school-ending hours, which creates hardships to supervise children at home. The "modern family" from the television show is what many families look like now, and that's great. I have no problem with who represents the family unit. What I have a problem with is the school thinking that children need to be at the school for nine-plus hours daily. With parents or guardians away from the home trying to make a living for the family, the children are left to either be at home alone, where they are unsupervised, or stay at school, where there is supervision and safety. This is a real dilemma that we need to solve.

Gradually school districts have taken on more and more of the role of parenting and daycare, meaning the children get to school early so they can have some breakfast and then stay until 4:30 or 5:00 for tutoring on schoolwork to make sure they get their needs met that normally would happen in the home.

The school districts have gone this direction because they feel like it's the only way that the students will learn to read, write, and do math as well as be supervised and remain safe. Over the past few years, this mentality has led to much more pressure from administrators and teachers for students to do well on a standardized test, increased pressure on teachers based on results of student's ability to pass standardized tests, and too much time for students sitting to prepare for a test that many of them will not do well on anyway.

As well, children are the most misbehaved we've ever seen. They lack focus. Many administrators are not supportive of the teacher's needs in the classroom. We have the largest classes we've ever seen and parents are more absent than ever, expecting more and more from the schools.

When parents don't like the results, many expect the school districts to change the rules for them. How has all of this worked for the educational system in the United States? We're no better off today than we were 30 years ago academically with this model of taking the kids on to raise. The students need more time away from the school setting on a daily basis in a different after-school environment.

The Finnish have an answer for this dilemma. Their system goes for quality within their school day and then sends the children home or to other places to be active and creative outside of the school setting. Once school is out, the students leave the campus for the most part to play or do something productive in a different environment. The students come back to school each day with a better outlook on school because they haven't spent all of their time there the day before and the day before that. All parents in the United States must take an active role in raising their children (reading with them, playing with them, and teaching them right from wrong).

Today's parents use technology to reach their children rather than actively engaging with their children. For example, the use of video games, television watching in the car, and social media engagement have altered the ability for the parent and child to interact in a meaningful way. U.S. schools need to move toward quality school days with high expectations and much less emphasis on teaching to a test. We need to remember that the other three aspects of the whole child (social, emotional, and physical) are just as important as one's cognitive ability.

We also need to give quality time to the arts, physical education, and unstructured outdoor play as part of the school day. When we can strike this balance, we will begin to see the teachers do what they do best, teach, and we will see the more productive results of learning that we have yearned to see over the past 30 years.

Here are some things to think about and problem solve.

The Finnish have a great public transportation system, and their schools are close enough for many students to walk home. If they want to go to a sports hall or a different place across town to do an activity, they just hop on the tram that connects all parts of the city. So it's easier for them to release their students to leave the campus earlier than when parents get home from work. The majority of the United States does not have this type of system in place. We need to find our own solutions for a balance between how long children should be in school and alternative programming off-site for after-school needs.

REFLECTION 12

EQUITY AND EXCELLENCE

Equity is defined as the quality of being fair and impartial. Excellence is defined as the quality of being outstanding. Both of these concepts have their place in societies across the world. The question is when different systems should focus on one or the other to create the most successful culture.

As this book is about comparing educational systems between Finland and America, this segment will focus on how these two countries use equity and excellence in their schools. Finland is known for its ability to create equity and excellence across its environment. To create equity, they provide fully subsidized meals, disability and special education services, and diverse learning environments in their classrooms for all students. They do not track or select certain students to be in specific classrooms or classes because of a diagnosis or assessment. They feel that, if they can educate every child in their country, then everyone will thrive in their environment.

This means that all children deserve the same education. All children learn in the same classrooms. No labels are given to separate students into different classrooms by content area. For example, in the United States, students may be classified in different ways based on an assessment or score of a certain classification type: honors, gifted and talented, and learning differences.

Each of these titles has expectations associated with it. Finland practices do not use these methods to place students in different types of classrooms. Rather, inclusive classroom and instructional efforts guide Finland's effort to minimize low achievement in their educational system. They also concentrate on a more cooperative classroom learning environment in the elementary school day that can be perceived as much less intense. They do not grade their students until after fifth grade.

Instead they use a developmental assessment by semester to send home progress for all of their students. Their days are much shorter than ours, ranging from grades one and two at four and a half hours daily to fifth grade at five and a half hours daily. They have 15 minutes of unstructured, outdoor play every hour of their school day. Once they reach grade six, the school/classroom environment begins to shift from cooperative to more competitive. Grading by content area, focusing on an assessment at the end of the compulsory school level (grade nine), and a more focused content expectation are all introduced at this level.

This is where the shift begins to happen with equity and excellence. By the time the students reach the secondary school experience, they are striving for excellence within the equitable environment that has been maintained for all of their compulsory years.

In contrast, the United States expects children to begin school at the preschool level (four to five years of age). Kindergarten is the first year all students begin a full day of school, which, on average, is a seven-hour day. Most public schools do not allow the young children to take naps, but they do offer snack time a couple of times daily. Outdoor play experiences are minimal, anywhere from no recess to indoor classroom activities for five-minute segments to substitute for the outdoor time daily. For some kindergarten classes, outdoor play doesn't happen until the afternoon, which is a long time for a young child to wait for physical activity and social time with their peers.

Teachers begin grading students early in the elementary school setting, but more importantly, benchmark tests and reading/math assessments begin in kindergarten and continue through the rest of the student's time in the K-12 setting in order to pass a standardized test each year beginning in third grade.

From a curriculum perspective, the Finnish educational governing body believes the teacher should have the freedom to teach the curriculum the way each wants to, but keeping all children equal in needs and meeting those needs. The objectives are established for each content area at each grade level. This means that the Finnish government determines through their education and culture department what objectives should be met at each grade level. These objectives are not cumbersome and are very reachable at each level. For example, in the crafts content area (working with wood in grade six), the students must be able to show an ability to work with the lathe at that age.

A class I observed was designing and building wooden cars with wooden, rounded wheels. The lathe was going to be used to make the wheels. Another class I observed was third grade learning about science. The teacher was teaching about insects. She was meeting the science objectives in her classroom with her 20 to 22 students her own way.

The teachers don't meet to discuss how they will teach the curriculum, when they will teach certain things, or how they will assess their students. They do meet occasionally to discuss how to reach certain children who are challenged by certain elements, but not how to teach in their classroom.

The teachers in Finland have quite a few freedoms without giving up equity. They have the freedom to schedule their classes within the time elements they choose each day, to leave when their last class is completed each day, and to assess their students individually but not comparatively. The principal does not watch over them or assess each of the teachers on the job they are doing. The principal trusts the teachers and knows that the teachers are doing what they are supposed to do.

How do they know? They have the cream of the crop teaching in the schools. They also know that a standardized test does not always capture what the students are learning in the classroom that contributes to the whole child (physical, social, emotional, and spiritual well-being).

In the United States, teachers do not have the same freedoms to teach that the Finnish teachers have. U.S. teachers are assessed by how well their students do on a test instead of how well adjusted the children are or how much they enjoy engaging in the learning experience. The curriculum that once was expected to be taught at the first-grade level is now curriculum expected to be taught at the kindergarten level or earlier.

Competition has become much more evident in early childhood. This is seen in labeling certain schools as better than others within the same school district, giving raises to teachers labelled as exceptional, and expecting children to learn objectives at earlier ages without consideration for child readiness in order to show we are the best in the world in academics.

Interestingly, the Finnish educational system preserves great teaching through requiring a written exam to enter a field of study and then limiting the number of individuals who can major in that specific content area. It's highly competitive to become a teacher, and a small percentage of individuals who apply are accepted in any given year to pursue a teacher education degree.

The curriculum at the university level is the same across universities for each content area. Teachers are taught and prepared the same way no matter which university they go to in Finland. So when the teachers graduate from the university with their master's degree, they all know how to teach, and they have spent many hours preparing to be teachers. Teaching in Finland is very well respected, and people want to be teachers in Finland. This way of preparing teachers is very different from the United States.

In the United States, there can be two paths to become a certified teacher. The most recognized and well-established path to become a teacher over the past one hundred years is through the university teacher education programs. Most of these programs are accredited through a national education group called Council for the Accreditation of Educator Preparation (CAEP), formerly known as the National Council for Accreditation of Teacher Education (NCATE) and the Teacher Education Accreditation Council (TEAC).[1]

A student entering college can choose to major in early childhood, elementary, and/or secondary teacher education with a designated content area, i.e., English, math, physical education. The student doesn't have to take an entrance exam or be chosen through a selection process to go this route. The accreditation boards require certain courses and internship experiences to be accomplished prior to receiving certification from the state of that university. For the most part, the student is receiving the necessary tools to be successful in a school setting.

The other path to become a certified teacher is what is called alternative teacher certification through other state-recognized organizations or educational region centers. A person taking this route is not required to take methodology courses in the content area to be certified. The interested individual only has to take a small number of education courses such as educational psychology and child development once demonstrating he or she has a qualified bachelor's degree in a specific content area.

There are definitely pros and cons to this type of teacher certification training. The difference is in how well teachers are respected who have been fully trained in teaching methodology versus those who might be trained in a field of study but may not know how to use proper methodology with individual learning needs.

The Finnish have mastered a balance between equity and excellence in education across diverse situations with students. This is something the United States definitely needs to work on. At this time, too much emphasis is placed on excellence in young children via assessments instead of focusing on the whole child in a much more collaborative manner.

Once we decide that a score does not truly reflect the cognitive abilities of children and begin to address the social, emotional, and physical elements of a child, children will begin to take an active role in learning again.

REFLECTION 13

EDUCATORS DEVELOPING INDEPENDENT THINKERS

As an athlete, one of the first things I learned was how to critique my own performance. It's one thing for others to tell you what you are doing right and wrong (constructive criticism), but mentors (coaches) always want to see the athletes grow so they can self-critique their performance and ultimately think/strategize on their feet when the coach isn't there as they become better athletes.

When I trained to become an educator, I took those same skills and applied them to my teaching performance. I had a mentor who gave me pointers, but ultimately, if I were going to be good at teaching, I needed to be able to self-reflect and make adjustments as they happened. It seemed very natural to me to be able to do this. Analyze what happened and then decide if I liked the outcome or if I needed to change something for the next time. This self-feedback has been key to my approach to life.

Is this really any different from what we should be doing to help our students in the K-12 setting do the same thing? Shouldn't our children be able to grow from the time they enter school to mature by high school into independent thinkers who know that certain decisions will make or break them for life? I feel that this is something that is missing from the educator's bag of tools in the United States.

This became very evident when I was conversing with a teacher at one of the elementary schools in Helsinki. This wasn't the first time I had heard these next few statements, but it was the first time I put the ideas together to realize one of the things we need to do a better job of in our U.S. schools is to develop independent thinkers.

One of the statements I heard was, "We have to allow our children to take a problem and solve it with the teacher as the mentor. We have to be able to give them a task to do and then let them work through it sometimes."

Another person stated, "We build success in our children when we see they are able to make good decisions and they see it worked."

When I reflect on observations I've seen in the Finland schools (university setting and grades one through nine), there is a common theme to give them a task and let them as a small group or in pairs work through it and come up with the best solution. It takes more time, but the Finnish pupil is still learning how to problem solve and make good decisions for the most part. The mentor (teacher/professor) will still give feedback (critique) as needed.

We need to remember that part: mentoring/educating is still needed. To let the child fail without feedback leads to more failure, very little problem solving, and ultimately quitting the task for good or bullying his or her way to a result he or she wants. Neither is the solution we should aim for.

I hope as we move forward as educators, we will remember that we need to develop independent thinkers. Allow the student to make mistakes, but mentor him or her to become self-evaluators through the process and eventually think independently with success. We want children who grow up to see the world with a critical eye, but an eye with the ability to create a picture with many lenses.

REFLECTION 14

LET'S NOT FORGET THE EDUCATIONAL STRENGTHS OF THE UNITED STATES

My objective from the beginning of planning the Finland trip was to learn from the Finnish educators about their strengths as an educational unit and bring those concepts back to the United States. In visiting with many people in Finland, including individuals from International Affairs, principals, teachers, and professors, I have confirmed what I already knew before embarking on this educational adventure: every country has a deep-seated culture that has many genuinely good qualities about it.

Until now, I have focused on the Finnish culture, educational system, and ways of life. A Finnish educator said to me, "Isn't it funny that it takes a person coming from another country to tell us (educators) that we are doing a great job?"

It made me realize that, although the United States wants to focus on the elements that will create better schools for all ages, we must also continue to recognize, support, and maintain the great things that our schools and teachers are doing. Below are some genuinely good qualities about the U.S. educational system that we should continue to support and strengthen.

1. Each state values the importance of certifying physical education teachers at all levels of the K-12 system.
2. Our universities prepare and our states certify excellent K-12 classroom (content) teachers whom our administrators need to trust are doing a great job.
3. We have specific master's degrees to become administrators and counselors in the schools.
4. We have all types of diversity, a strength that we must embrace in our schools. It's what has created the U.S. cultural identity.
5. We have great opportunities to do and be what we want to be. We need to make sure all children know and feel this is possible.
6. We offer study abroad programs for our students to see the world from different perspectives.

As much as we strive for academic excellence through our policies and procedures presently, we have lost sight of the whole child's needs. It wasn't too long ago that we knew how to cultivate the whole child in our schools. Finnish educators have learned systematically from the United States and other countries how to reform education and improve teaching in schools. The United States has been a special source of inspiration to Finland since John Dewey almost a century ago.

John Dewey[1] believed learning was active and schooling unnecessarily long and restrictive. His idea was that children came to school to do things and live in a community that gave them real, guided experiences that fostered their capacity to contribute to society. Such American educational innovations as cooperative learning, problem-based teaching, and experiential learning, especially outdoors, are examples of the practices invented by teachers and researchers in the United States that over the past thirty years have become common practices in the Finnish classroom.

The difference is that Finland realizes that these practices are very important to healthy learning and protecting those educational elements above and beyond any other changes they implement. Conversely, we have moved further away from Dewey's principles and a developmental learning environment. There are specific developmental principles such as play and content readiness that have been dismissed in schools in our race to be the best across the globe. It's all about creating the best learning environment for our schools (teachers and students). Our culture is rich with diversity and opportunity. We must recognize the elements we once had, which Finland found productive for educating children that will help us once again be at the top of our game for generations to come.

REFLECTION 15

MOVEMENT IS THE KEY TO LEARNING

From the time children in Finland go to school, the teachers emphasize moving as part of the curriculum—not only as a content area (physical education) but also as part of their other content classroom time. Children in Finland can start school in the year that they turn seven. Before that, a child may take one year of preschool. Preschool is designed to develop creative skills whether it be through movement, art, music, or crafts.

All children are required to attend school, which is a compulsory education system. This means they must attend from the age of seven through the end of basic education (grade nine) or no more than ten years after starting their compulsory education. The pupil can then apply for advanced education.

The Finnish school system truly emphasizes movement throughout this compulsory education time period. They believe this helps the students stay motivated and grasp different concepts.

In week three, I observed a daycare facility where the Finnish begin their journey in a public setting to create movement in their children's lives. This sets the scene for going to school where they will continue this pattern. These children were about five years of age and were engaging in an hour of activity and storytelling with a group of students from the University of Helsinki early childhood program.

The university students worked up a story about a troll and the different experiences related to the forest that would eventually lead the children to the troll's mother who needed to be freed from a tree. The little children collected different objects at each station they went to and experienced all kinds of things related to their senses (smell, sight, and touch). They also found different objects around the forest area to add to their bag of collected items.

At the end, they used little keys to unlock the troll's mother from the tree. The children took turns freeing her and feeling good about all they had done in that hour. They were moving, focusing, and listening all the time. It was great to see the children doing such fun activities and enjoying the forest setting behind their school.

I know that teachers and parents in the United States want more movement in the schools just like Finland has. I wish state and federal educational agencies, as well as some school personnel who make school-wide decisions, would recognize how important movement is to the brain function and learning of students. Students in America will continue to struggle academically if the school day continues to get longer. Especially for younger children, success of learning is based on a standardized test score, and the most important focus in a school day is academics. Very little consideration is given to the social, emotional, and physical development of the child.

REFLECTION 16

SPORTS, PHYSICAL ACTIVITY, AND CULTURE–THE VISION

The third week was full of many different facets of experiences related to the Finnish educational system. I started off Monday observing in a traditional grade one through six school. I spent Tuesday and Wednesday at a grade one through nine school. Thursday, I was at Espoo, a city outside of Helsinki, with the preschool children in the forest, and Friday, I was at the Finnish Sports Federation (FSF) site.

The appointment with the FSF was interesting because I only understood the U.S. sport perspective until then. In the United States, we have so many different elements related to sport from pee wee programs to youth sport programs, competitive school athletics, university athletic programs, club teams at the preadolescent through college levels, adult sport leagues, and finally professional sports. They are not all under the same umbrella. In Finland, they are.

The FSF is multifaceted. Their main goal is to connect sport and physical activity to the community across the life span. They believe everyone should have the opportunity to exercise and do sports from all angles. The FSF, in partnership with the Finnish Broadcasting Company (YLE) for over two years, shared an objective to find new techniques both for activating those who have not exercised and enhance a sense of community through physical activity and sport.

What came of this was Vision 2020, which states that the "Finnish will be the most physically active sports nation in the world." They feel their role is to be the leader and coordinator of the many collaborative groups who will make this possible: professional sports teams, the Finnish Olympic Committee, Finnish Paralympic Committee, and sector-specific groups (children, youth, and adults).

The FSF is focused on the whole life span. The Finns have developed a branch of the FSF called Young Finland, focused primarily on children, founded as its own entity in 1993. This association's purpose is to integrate more physical activity into the pupil's school and after-school day. Their objective is to increase the pupil's will to exercise, create equality and attention for all, build honesty and open-mindedness, introduce a balance of nature, and develop solid social skills.

Young Finland, with a staff of about 30, has concentrated on several concepts: being physically active, eating right, getting nine to ten hours of sleep, and limiting sedentary behavior. The following are some of the things they have promoted and emphasized through media outlets: that any pupil between the ages of seven and eighteen should be physically active for at least one to two hours daily and should sit less than two hours at any given time within the day. Another emphasis of the program is to train peer instructors from grades five through nine to work with the younger children. In the older grades, they have also influenced the schools to have at least one long recess per day of 30 minutes, whereas the other recesses required each hour are 15 minutes each. I observed the pupils through a cycle of content classes and recesses and understand why they want one longer recess per day.

Their newest national action program devised to activate physical activity across all children in their schools is Finnish Schools on the Move[1] (https://liikkuvakoulu.fi/english). This program has been initiated by the Ministry of Education and Culture with the key objective of ensuring a minimum of sixty minutes of physical activity in the schools each day for all children. The promotion of physical activity among school-aged children consists of both increasing physical activity and decreasing sedentary time. This requires measures to be undertaken at school and at home.

The actions they suggest are increasing the number of physical education lessons weekly, promoting active commuting between school and home, and implementing active learning methods in the classroom, which will decrease excessive sitting during school lessons.

The observations I made when watching each recess is the pupils would go out independently of one another from their classes and some would begin instantly playing different activities (soccer, tag, stand-up scooters, or an activity called *diabolo*[2]). Many others would stand and visit for the first five minutes and then begin to break up into groups to play activities. It was interesting to watch this because it happened every recess that way. When the longer 25 to 30 minute recess was offered for the older kids, they really could engage in more physical activity than with a 15 minute time period.

I feel that a couple of things that were stressed during this observation are important to their way of working sports into the culture.

1. They don't want sport to consume the younger child; they want it to be an avenue for being active regularly.
2. They want activity or gym areas to be accessible for all ages who want to be active and can't afford to pay for access. Many of the sports will cost to participate, but there are some offered

that children can participate free or with a minimal charge (like two euros per session).

This goes back to the equality emphasis that I have stressed previously, which they are now emphasizing with sport as well. The government has given funds to the sports club budgets to be able to help children participate without fees for some of the sports.

The United States has a very complex system for sport, and trying to have one federation that controls all of it is virtually impossible. I do, however, support a less competitive sport environment for children. In elementary grade levels, sports should only be introduced in physical education classes with the purpose of developing motor skills and promoting regular physical activity.

REFLECTION 17

JYVÄSKYLÄ, WHERE CERTIFIED PE HAPPENS

Faculty 1 coordinated efforts for me to visit and observe in the city north of Helsinki called Jyväskylä. This is a beautiful place in the fall with all of the colors I was able to experience. This is the only university in Finland that trains physical education (PE) teachers.

What does this really mean? Content teachers (responsible for thirteen subject areas) teach physical education (as one of the content areas) in the elementary schools. In order to teach physical education as your only content area, you must have a master's degree in physical education. This is required to teach in the lower secondary schools (grades seven through nine) and the upper secondary schools (university prep and vocational prep high schools).

Certified physical educators do not teach in the elementary schools usually. Typically, a classroom teacher (who has a master's in education and might have a specialization in PE) will teach PE in the elementary school setting. That's not always the case though. Teachers with no PE specialization will also teach PE at the elementary level.

Since this is the only university to train physical education teachers, it is highly competitive to become a specialized teacher for PE. Only 80 students (5 percent of the total number of applicants applying to the physical education program) are accepted yearly for this degree, and all of them will earn jobs when they graduate.

Interestingly, there are 2,500 physical education teachers in the country for which these new graduates will be hired into the system at either the lower secondary or high school levels predominately. These teachers are highly respected, and when polled, Mäkelä and colleagues[1] found that 80 percent of PE teachers were satisfied or extremely satisfied with their work and that 74 percent of the graduated PE teachers were still teaching PE at the schools some 20 years later.

I would like to guide you through the process that it takes to be accepted into the University of Jyväskylä's PE program. The selection process is rigorous and undoubtedly is why PE teachers are so well respected and have such credibility in the schools.

The first phase is for the selection committee to examine the pool of applicants and consider four criteria: initial entry points, matriculation exam grades, high school grades, and previous studies of tertiary level.

For example, a recent year's student pool applying for the physical education degree was 1,600 in Phase 1, which was then narrowed down to 360 men and women for Phase 2. And finally 50 men and women would be selected to begin the physical education major.

Once Phase 1 is completed, the second phase is to take the 180 men and 180 women selected from the 1,600 and put them through a three-day selection process of exams (which has been done like this since the 1960s). They are tested on a micro teaching lesson, a test of writing competency, and tests of motor skills. These tests require 10 hours a day of rigorous skills for that three-day process.

From there, the selection of 25 males and 25 females takes place for enrollment in the PE program at the university.

There are two alternative ways a student can be accepted into the University of Jyväskylä:

1. They are already teaching (about 400 in Finland) and do not have their master's degree in PE. In this case, they are applying to come back to earn it.
2. The other group to be accepted has gone the vocational degree route and now is coming back to be a physical education teacher.

A total of no more than 30 will be accepted from one of these two routes, still going through the same rigor as explained above.

I learned the following over a two-day period at this university:

- Each faculty mentor takes a group of 10 to 20 students each year and teaches them all of their PE classes for the five-year degree period, which is a 3-2 program like we have in the United States. The difference is the same mentor stays with this group for the whole process.
- Reflection is huge for student learning in this five-year process. This means that the students should be able to develop their professional knowledge from their own professional experiences.
- They have lots of field experiences from year one through year five.
- They become very confident to teach by the time they enter the teaching profession.
- There are no shortcuts!
- Faculty are highly invested in these students throughout their time at the university.
- The students commute by bicycle most of the time, even in snow. They change out their tires to snow tires.

This section demonstrates the rigor of PE training for secondary teachers in Finland. I think we have many PE certification programs in the United States that put our students through rigor. The U.S. university system has very few programs that put the incoming physical education students through the testing rigor to be accepted into the programs as the Finns.

We must remember that in order to be respected in the United States like the Finnish, we must apply rigor to our physical education programs as well. Mediocrity should not be tolerated, and teaching PE should be a privilege awarded to the best of our university students. Let's ensure our students earn the right to be physical education teachers through rigorous university certification programs.

Alternative programs should be eliminated or required to meet similar standards the university programs are held to. Our school children deserve this from us. On another note, that means the PE teachers we have in the secondary schools should already be teaching PE extremely well. The community and administrators in the schools should expect that of our PE teachers.

REFLECTION 18

THE GERM

I have mentioned previously a leader in the Finland education reform over the past few years who has helped Finland be a country that others want to emulate. I have explained in earlier reflections the U.S. school problems and the need to problem solve new ways to correct them. A leader in the educational reform of Finland is Dr. Pasi Sahlberg.[1] He has eloquently written about why countries across the globe are sick and lacking the tools to succeed. He calls it the Global Educational Reform Movement, or GERM.[2] It's a virus epidemic that has spread and infected education systems through media, politicians, and experts in the field with infected opinions. He believes the GERM has impacted the United States, just as it has other major educational players such as China and Japan.

How is the virus spread? Education systems borrow policies and procedures from each other that spread the virus to schools. As a result, the schools become a toxic environment where teachers don't feel well and kids learn less. Interestingly, Dr. Sahlberg explains that the GERM infection has three major symptoms: more competition within education systems, increased school choice, and stronger accountability from schools and related standardized testing of students.

For the first symptom, he states many reformers believe that the quality of education improves when schools compete against one another. In order to compete, reformers feel that schools need more autonomy, which means more accountability. This equates to school inspections, standardized testing, and teacher effectiveness evaluations.

The U.S. schools are doing exactly this and suffering as a result. We have lost the ability to cooperate and continue to compete with each other in order to be the best. Even within a school district, schools place banners on their school walls stating they are better than other schools in their own district, teachers compete for awards, and standardized testing has become a required practice for students across all grade levels (upwards of 20 yearly).

The United States, through the Obama era and into the Trump presidency, continue to push for school choice. This is the second symptom of the GERM. As Sahlberg states,

> It essentially positions parents as consumers empowering them to select schools for their children from several options and thereby promotes market-style competition into the system as schools seek to attract those parents. More than two-thirds of Organization for Economic Co-operation and Development (OECD)[3] countries have increased school choice opportunities for families with the perceptions that market mechanisms in education would allow equal access to high-quality schooling for all. Increasing numbers of charter schools in the United States, secondary school academies in England, free schools in Sweden and private schools in Australia are examples of expanding school choice policies. Yet according to the OECD, nations pursuing such choice have seen both

a decline in academic results and an increase in school segregation.

U.S. parents and educators are very aware of the sickness related to the third GERM symptom, standardized testing. According to the Center for Public Education,[4] standardized testing has increased teaching to the test, narrowed curricula to prioritize reading and mathematics, and distanced teaching from the art of pedagogy to mechanistic instruction. It has also led to less creativity, problem solving, and critical thinking skills. Students regurgitate material and no longer think about how they can make a difference in the world. They just want to know the answer.

Healthy school systems like Finland are resistant to the GERM and its inconvenient symptoms.

Dr. Sahlberg has explained the GERM well. Education leaders in America need to revisit these policies and disinfect the schools from these symptoms if we are to become a healthy and productive educational setting again. Read more about the GERM at www. pasisahlberg.com/blog.[2]

REFLECTION 19

SECONDARY EDUCATION IN FINLAND

I haven't talked much about the secondary level of education and especially physical education in the Finnish schools. The Finns place a lot of emphasis on early childhood and elementary education. This is where habits are formed and learning as a skill is established. They want to firmly build the foundation so students can be successful when they enter the secondary level and ultimately succeed as adults. The Finns believe, as the Americans do, that the more educated their population is, the better the people will function and contribute to the society. The difference is they really create an atmosphere for this to happen for the majority of their students.

As a review, basic education includes grades one through nine. Then the secondary level divides into vocational or general upper secondary schools. Students have to apply for these studies through a joint application system while they are in the ninth grade of basic education. The selection of students for upper secondary school is based on their grade point average for the theoretical subjects in the basic education certificate. Entrance and aptitude tests may also be used, and students may be awarded points for hobbies and other relevant activities. Either route of high school training usually takes three more years to complete and gives eligibility for higher education.

At the vocational institutes, students can study a wide variety of subjects based on their own interests. The most popular fields of study are technology, communications, transport and social services, health, and sports. Applicants must take a language skills exam before being accepted by the vocational upper secondary school. Once accepted, the studies will emphasize practical skills, which include on-the-job training. This route is popular with more than 40 percent of the relevant age group entering into the vocational upper secondary school immediately after basic education. After completing the studies, graduates can start working in their trained field or continue on to an institute of higher education (if accepted).

For the general upper secondary school option, the students prepare for further studies at a university or university of applied sciences. Both higher education structures have their own profiles. Universities emphasize scientific research and teaching, whereas universities of applied sciences adopt a more practical approach. There is restricted entry into all fields of study at the higher education level. Due to the high volume of applicants for the limited number of places available in higher education, a matriculation exam or entrance test is the most common measure used for acceptance into one of these programs.

This exam is very lengthy (three full days) and can be taken sometime in their third year of high school. The secondary schools will schedule specific times in the fall or spring for each student to complete his or her exams. The students spend most days leading up to the exam in preparation. More about the education options can be found at https://www.oph.fi/english/education_system/basic_education.

The Finns have an educational plan that not only builds intrinsic motivation and confidence in the students from early childhood on, but by the time they need to consider high school, they feel like they can pass the exams. The 2016 statistics for Finnish students show more than 98 percent of six-year-olds attend preschool classes since the students do not begin the primary school until age seven. Ninety-nine percent of the students complete compulsory basic education, and 94 percent of those who start the academic strand of upper secondary school graduate (https://www.stat.fi/til/kou_en.html).

Completion rates in vocational upper secondary school also reach close to 90 percent (https://www.stat.fi/til/kou_en.html). If a student does not receive a secondary-level placement after completing comprehensive school (because they failed their exams), they offer a tenth year for students to address the subject area weaknesses they have and then apply again for a high school program (vocational or upper secondary). Students may also include an introduction to different vocational fields and upper secondary studies during this tenth year. The student will take part in the joint application system again at the end of the tenth year. There are other ways individuals can be coached into the secondary educational system, but this is the one that applies to the majority of students.

The Finns have stated repeatedly that there is no dead end for a student who wants to be more educated and complete higher level coursework. A student may do the vocational institute and then decide he or she wants to pursue a university degree. Students can pursue different studies at that point if they are accepted into the program. The university programs are highly competitive, and students have to be at the top of their game to be admitted and to succeed with a degree.

What I've learned from this culture is that, because they create a standard of acceptance into high school, students really prepare and focus on getting into a high school program. It's a great concept. The European philosophy in general adopts this mind-set. Each country does things a little different, but in general, it's competitive, and an exam separates those who enter high school and those who don't.

REFLECTION 20

GET OUTSIDE—NO BOX REQUIRED

I have reflected on many observations at this point and feel that the Finnish have mastered the way they live through the outdoors. There are many opportunities for Americans to get outside and enjoy the surroundings through biking, hiking, kayaking, snow skiing, and so on, and many Americans in different states do take advantage from an exercise perspective.

As much opportunity as there is in some places to enjoy activity, there are many reasons Americans don't do more of it, in fact any at all. One is the technology craze: TV, computer games, searching the web, and even exercise with computer programs (like Wii programs). Not only are all of these things inside activities, they are for the most part sedentary activities.

Second is the safety issue. Many people feel they can't go outside to participate in activities because someone might shoot or kidnap them. Third is the lack of biking/walking trails for commuting in many areas of the United States. I think programs like Rails to Trails is a great way of creating long-distance biking/walking trails by turning railroad trails that are never used into these types of trails.

Even if people wanted to use forms of exercise as ways to

commute, it is very difficult because of the lack of trails to get where they need to go. Fourth is the fast pace of the American society. I have been very active in Finland, but when I'm back in Texas, I'm just like everyone else. I jump in the car to run to the grocery store that is only one to two miles away. Why don't I walk to the store? It takes time that I don't feel I have when I'm in work mode.

Most Americans feel this way as well. They will jump in the car to do everything instead of jumping on a bike or walking to pick up something or commute to their jobs. Fifth is that Americans have become a very lazy society. We have cars, remotes, and internet for everything so we never need to get up to go anywhere. We can sit and get everything done. As overweight as our society is becoming, we still would rather try shortcuts (a pill, a surgery, or a diet) to change instead of doing the hard work of being physically active.

The Finns take the exercise concept to an all new level. Finns don't just exercise in workout facilities or at home. They are outside all the time. Outdoor recreation is the Finnish way of life. It's not just about exercise. It's about who they are and how they live life. Ninety-seven percent of Finnish people participate in outdoor activities on a regular basis. The most popular physical activities are walking, swimming in natural waters, bicycling, and cross-country skiing.

What is more amazing is that they begin this mind-set with their children very early on. Since the parents are active outside, they take their children with them to be active. Then when school starts for children at the age of seven, all recess activity is outside until it reaches minus 15 degrees Celsius. Otherwise, the children are required to go outside to play and be active. They dress for the conditions and deal with it. This means the teachers who supervise also go outside with them and remain out there for each of the recess periods. More of the physical education classes are outside as well. They use the indoor facilities when they do an indoor-type sport only (floor hockey). If given the chance though, they would rather play outside than inside.

I have experienced this way of life myself now. Before I came over here to observe and learn, I didn't understand this mentality. I had my restrictions on when I would go outside and how long I would be out there (too windy, too hot, too cold, or looking like it wanted to rain).

In Finland, especially during this time of year (fall), it is gray and overcast most of the time. You could get rained on any time. You never know when it might strike. I realized that in order to observe the physical education and recess times, I had to go outside, no matter the conditions, and I would be out there for three to four hours in a row with different classes.

I would be bundled up with a scarf around my neck, gloves, long johns, lined pants, two shirts, warm-up jacket, and a Gore-Tex jacket. Wouldn't you think I would be warm enough? The wind can make it feel fairly cold here. I started getting conditioned to this weather and started going out in the elements no matter whether it might rain or not, whether it was colder or not, and whether I had time or not.

I started enjoying the different types of weather and began feeling like the colder temperatures and rain were no big deal. I began to realize why the Finnish people ride their bikes and walk even when it is pouring down rain. It's their way of life. They think that everything should be outside.

When I was in Jyväskylä, I saw how many bikes are used all around the city. I said to one of the faculty I was walking with that I guess they would quit riding when it began to snow.

She said, "No, they would just change their tires to snow tires."

I didn't know they had them. That is such a different way of thinking. The Finns really capitalize on being active and especially outdoors. Nothing gets in their way.

We need to build more paths for people to use for commuting

in the United States. We need more parks and recreational areas closer to all neighborhoods. We also need to have an activity mind-set instead of an exercise mind-set. I agree with the Finns that we need to be moving more than one hour at the beginning or end of each day. We need to make moving part of the majority of our day. No more than two hours at any given time sitting or being sedentary.

Let's start being more like that. Our obesity rates will begin to drop if we begin to move more often throughout the day. Let's start doing more of our physical education classes outside as well. Children need the outdoors. It really does improve the emotional and physical dimensions of the person. Get outside! No box required!

REFLECTION 21

ETHICAL DILEMMA

I had observed a lot of different classroom and gym settings over the past few weeks in Finland. I am always in amazement at how attentive, focused, and respectful these pupils were in Finland. I'd also observed many different classrooms and gym settings over the past few years in the United States. I am always in amazement at how many of the students lack attention, focus, and respect for anyone or anything.

Where have things gone wrong? I've said for many years that the pendulum has been swinging the wrong direction. I feel that there are some issues that have brought us to this place.

The Finns have maintained certain principles since becoming their own country again and will not compromise those principles for anyone. They will be fair and treat everyone equally without compromising their standards. One of the basic principles included as a content area within their curriculum is ethics or religion. When children enter school at age seven, the parents will decide whether the child will take religion or ethics. The religions generally offered in the schools are Lutheran (the predominant religion in Finland), Greek Orthodox, Catholic, Jewish, and Muslim. If two or more students belong to a different religion, they can request to have a priest or minister from that religion come in to teach the class. If only one student belongs to a specific religion, he or she will have to take the ethics class. There are no exceptions. All students in Finland will take one or the other class.

I sat in on an ethics class. I was very impressed with the topics that were addressed. For example, the students were given an assignment to do research on something that is design-oriented in Finland and decide if that design piece is ethical and why. One of the students who speaks fairly good English was asked to share her PowerPoint presentation with me regarding this assignment. She was a fifth grader who had done a remarkable job on the PowerPoint slides. I couldn't believe the aesthetic quality of the slides, much less the content on each.

A couple of things that she said really made me think. She had picked a jacket-type piece of clothing to discuss. It was very stylish, would have covered the body well, and had great lines. Her standards for what would make it ethical were the following:

- It needed to be made by an adult from Finland with materials from Finland.
- It should not be made by a child over the adult or from someone who works as cheap labor.
  This tells me a few things:
- She has been taught through the ethics class that adults should be respected.
- Their work should be purchased over a child's work.
- People should not be asked to work for little or nothing.
- Finland products should be respected and chosen over other countries' products.

I really can't believe how much these students critically think about different issues and can verbalize and write it so well.

Another topic discussed was emotional abuse. They had to

identify forms of emotional abuse and then decide if emotional abuse was worse than physical abuse. This is a very good topic to develop in these children's minds this early in life. Bullying is one of the top emotional abuses discussed globally these days, and the students wrote about it in their journals that day. The student I was talking with stated that emotional abuse is much worse than physical abuse because it can stay with you longer and scar you for life.

At least once a month, the teacher-directed topics are generated from the UN website. The website always announces different days to celebrate or recognize. The abuse topic came from that website. This is a great way to teach children to be respectful of each other and their elders, both physically and emotionally.

I feel the United States has lost its way on what is right and what is wrong. We have clouded our existence as a nation with trying to be fair to everyone. We can be fair without losing the basic principles that have made us who we are today. We were built on religion, ethics, and a moral compass. Having ethical standards for many years was taught through religion in the United States. Since visiting a church regularly seems to have lost its roots with many families these days, teaching ethics or character skills should be a requirement in the U.S. schools to develop that moral compass again.

Our classes are full of students today who do not respond well to authority; nor do they care what anyone thinks about them. That is a sure-fire recipe for disaster. Our students are just as bright as other students across the globe. Let's start teaching all of our children to be empathetic, responsible, focused, respectable, and all-around good citizens. This will help them to be good learners and stewards of our society.

REFLECTION 22

SANTA SIGHTING AT THE NORTH POLE

Did you know that Santa lives in Finland up in the Arctic Circle in Rovaniemi? If you look on a map, you will see Rovaniemi is located in the northern part of Finland, which is where the North Pole is. His post office is there where he receives all of your mail for your wishes and gift lists. His elves live there too. The reindeer are taken care of, and you will actually see him taking rides in the forests on his sleigh every so often as well.

In the wintertime, a huge ice house and ice bar are built for the people to enjoy who come up to see Santa. He stays busy year-round, and you are more than welcome to visit him if you are in the area. It's about an hour flight from Helsinki to Rovaniemi where he resides. You could also take a train overnight if that suits you better. If you are in the area, it's a great adventure and definitely worth your time to see.

Here's a little history about Santa's place at Rovaniemi.[1]

About a hundred years ago, a passerby started spreading the word about Ear Mountain and the existence of its inhabitants. Santa wanted to safeguard the tranquility of his secret hiding place and came up with a superb idea that also allowed him to meet people who love Christmas and his many friends who come to greet him. It was around a half-century ago that Santa Claus started to frequently visit the Arctic Circle near Rovaniemi.

From the turn of the millennium, the Lappish center for Christmas, the Santa Claus Village on the Arctic Circle, became the most spectacular Santa Claus destination in Scandinavia. The popularity of the destination saw the number of visitors double. The number of international visitors in particular increased up to fourfold in a few years to exceed a half million. If you are interested in visiting or learning more, the website address is www. santaclausvillage.info/

REFLECTION 23

THE FINNISH NATIONAL AGENCY FOR EDUCATION

I met with Finland's secretary of education this past week. He has a heart for getting kids moving. His background is physical education, and his predominant role is physical education with the Finnish National Agency for Education.[1] He gave some basic statistics about Finland that I have compared below to the United States.

Finland Statistics
Independent since 1917
Total area: 338,000 square kilometers (130,128 square miles)
Population: 5.5 million people
Two official languages: Finnish and Swedish
Religion: Lutheran
United States Statistics[2]
Independent since 1776
Total area: 9.83 million square kilometers (3.80 million square miles)
Population: 325 million

Official language: None. Although English is spoken most often, many languages are spoken in the United States.

Religion: None. (Many are represented, although Protestant and Catholic are the most practiced.)

Finland as a country is much smaller than most states in the United States, but has a powerful punch when it comes to educating their students. If we are going to identify ways we can better ourselves academically and we want to follow basic principles that Finland has established, then we must examine how different states can make changes, not just the United States as a whole. A focus of many in education long term is to see improved high school graduation rates and retention of students (less dropouts).

The U.S. high school graduation rate is ranked 22nd out of 26 developed countries. Finland and Japan are tied for second for the top graduation rates. The US Institute of Education Sciences (IES)[3] reported high school graduation rates at around 84 percent in 2016, whereas in 2011, the rates were at 74 percent. Finland graduates around 94 percent each year from their upper secondary (high school) programs consistently.

Although U.S. high school graduation rates have been reported as increasing since 2011, there are still concerns with the percentages reported. Some critics believe that grades have been inflated and graduation requirements have been relaxed in many areas of the country so that students' graduation rates from high school will look better.

Michael Cohen,[4] president of Achieve, a national nonprofit that long advocated for higher standards and graduation rates states, "You don't know how many students who were in that graduation rate actually completed a rigorous course of study. We're not transparent about that. We're concealing a problem."

About 10 percent of our students can compete globally and show outstanding results against the other top countries. The problem is the other 90 percent can't. When foreign exchange students come to the United States, 85 percent say their U.S. classes were easier than classes in their native country. Finland and others understand that quality education is the path to a middle class.

"If you were running a grocery store instead of a school and you saw every day thirty out of a hundred customers leave your store without buying anything year after year, day after day, you would start to change your inventory."

This problem also shows up when a student who graduates from high school cannot complete the first year at a community college because he or she still can't read or write. The dropout rate at the college level for first-year students is 35 percent.[4] We have got to quit inflating numbers just to see a student receive a high school diploma. American schools have a much bigger problem than graduation and dropout rates.

Shouldn't we think about changing the way we educate our students? Finland's secretary of education continued to emphasize that the Finnish education system has many ways to complete an education. They emphasize a vocational track and a university track. The United States has de-emphasized vocational tracks over the past thirty years. More and more pressure is placed on American students to graduate from high school and go directly into a university setting. Statistics from countries like Finland who have vocational and university high school tracks show that having these choices is very successful for overall student success.

The Finns truly believe that the more education a person has, the more successful he or she will be and will, in turn, build a strong middle class for their country. The United States needs to focus more on offering high school vocational tracks in the curriculum to help students feel good about the path of interest they want to pursue and then requiring a passing grade on an exam to enter a vocational school for their college training. Not all students are cut out for going to a four-year university and majoring in something that means nothing to them. Jobs can be acquired by training from different angles. A vocational track is another way to do it.

The secretary of education also believes that physical activity and physical education should continue to be main content emphases in the schools. He wants to continue building recess and physical education time into the school day. This would be in vocational and university-prepared high schools. Physical education is ranked third behind math and Finnish as the most hours emphasized per week for content across the curriculum in Finland. He has been a huge advocate for the physical education requirement over time in the curriculum. We need educational leader's voices at the federal and state levels like his to help get people moving again and advocating for different types of high schools (vocational versus university).

The model that the Finnish education system uses is on the next page.[1] I hope this helps you to see how there are no dead ends to be educated to the fullest extent.

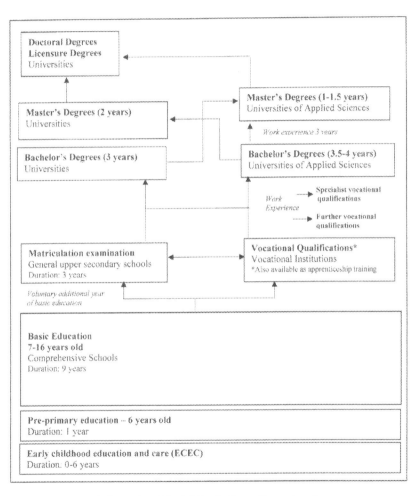

Education Model Path from Preschool
through Post-Graduate Degrees

REFLECTION 24

ARE ETHICS AND RELIGION PART OF THE SOLUTION?

I still truly believe one of the most pivotal pieces to improving our ability to educate and children's ability to learn is to teach character in the schools. I feel that we need to get a grasp on what is essential to the betterment of people and treating everyone with respect and dignity without losing the basic principles of right and wrong. In Finland, ethics and religion are emphasized in schools. We don't have to adopt their way of teaching what I consider to be good character skills, but I think we do need to know why they emphasize both.

What are the differences between ethics and religion? Finland teaches both. I visited with two of the University of Helsinki faculty who prepare students to be ethics or religion content specialists in the schools. They gave their thoughts on this topic of teaching ethics or religion and why each would be important.

Let's consider differences between ethics and religion as discussed by the two professors and some of the websites I've listed at the end of this segment.

Ethics is internal. The word *ethics* comes from the Greek root, *ethos*, which means character or habit. To act ethically is to do what is right. To act unethically is to do what is wrong. Of course, standards of right and wrong may vary by country. Ethics can be defined as the study and practice of morality that influences the beliefs and actions of individuals, communities, and societies.

Religion is external. The word *religion* comes from the Latin root, *religio*, meaning reverence. Religion refers to organized methods of worship. Religion seeks to answer questions of transcendence, such as "Why am I alive? What is my purpose? What is my relationship to higher realities or beings?" The three major religions of the world—Christianity, Judaism, and Islam—are structures that serve to organize not only groups of believers, but also their beliefs.

We are faced with ethical dilemmas daily. Do you pocket the $100 bill you found in the restroom at the restaurant? Will you get to work an hour early tomorrow to make up for today's long lunch break? Each individual's moral compass is what guides his or her behavior. The ethicist's initial concern focuses on the morality of individuals.

People can be religious and unethical or vice versa. You might know someone who faithfully goes to church, ministers to people in need, and prays fervently. You might be surprised to find out the person also has a gambling addiction. On the other hand, you might know someone who is honest to a fault, respects humanity, and gives to great causes, but has never been to a church or been associated with a religion. Religion is the body while ethics is the soul. The religious person attempts to ascertain the root of morality, that is, one's relationship to higher realities, forces, or beings.

Finnish children attend the same schools and classes regardless of their family's background, wealth, or culture. However, for one subject a week, children are divided into groups by religion or ethics if they don't have a specific religion.

How can you teach religion in school when children come

from increasingly diverse homes? Should society be responsible for providing children with instruction in religion? How can you guarantee fairness, equality, and level of instruction?

These questions are being discussed in Finland and all over Europe. Just a few decades ago, nearly all Finns were members of the Finnish Evangelical Lutheran Church, but a significant minority of today's pupils are nonreligious or belong to another religion. At the same time, the state's relationship with the Evangelical Lutheran Church and, representing the traditional minority, the Finnish Orthodox Church, have dissolved, and society has become secularized.

The relationship between education and religion incites strong feelings. When Finland's Freedom of Religion Act was amended in 2003, the legislative process included extensive debate regarding teaching religion in school. Those holding fast to traditional values demanded the preservation of denominational religious instruction, whereas more radical elements felt that religious instruction should be eliminated altogether.

The compromise resulted in the concept of *instruction in one's own religion*, which strives to guarantee the rights of minorities and to ensure that the child receives an education in accordance with his or her family's convictions. Nonreligious pupils study a subject called Life Perspective Studies, which includes ethics, worldview studies, and comparative religion.

The Finnish compromise stems from the fact that teaching is not denominational, but rather respects the child's personal background. Religion as a mandatory subject is still considered necessary because it supports development of the child's own identity and worldview, which also establishes a foundation for an intercultural dialogue.

Because Finland has been homogeneously Evangelical Lutheran since the Reformation, it would be difficult to understand the country's society and culture without knowing the history and thinking of the Lutheran church.

The goal of a religious curriculum is to familiarize pupils with their own religion and the Finnish traditions of belief, acquaint students with other religions, and help them understand the cultural and human significance of religions. A key part of religious instruction is dealing with ethical issues in a way that is appropriate to children.

The two professors stated that teaching religion approaches the curriculum from a narrative perspective: they can identify different people and situations throughout history that have changed the way we see life. The teacher should then present these different stories in the curriculum and weave a learning environment that is conducive for moral development. They would say that teaching ethics is about leading discussions on the issues. It is up to the student/pupil to come up with the answers to these issues and for the teacher to be able to help him or her see the right and wrong in the issue but not damage the child with his or her own opinions.

They both felt that the teacher needs to be very competent in ethics or religion (whichever he or she is teaching). A teacher who is not very competent in using this curriculum will have problems with conceptual theories and lessons. They both believe that these concepts should be practiced over and over with others who are learning these methods before teaching in the schools.

This reflection has highlighted what religion and ethics are. It has also examined why Finland finds it so important to teach religion or ethics in their schools. This is a very important time in the United States to consider what is most important for children in schools and how much of a role social/emotional learning should play in our K-12 schools. Public schools used to be a much different learning environment when empathy, expectations, trust, honesty, and respect were at the forefront.

Presently in many schools across the country, the classroom is chaotic, unfocused, disrespectful, and all about "me." Focusing on a character development curriculum taught for a few minutes daily in the schools, along with more outdoor physical activity time, could set up a better foundation for learning and less burnout by the time children reach third grade.

Read more from this Finland website if interested.

http://finland.fi/Public/default.aspx?contentid=190181&nodeid=41800&culture=en-US

REFLECTION 25

QUALITY VS. QUANTITY (THE GERM MIND-SET)

These Finland experiences have led me to think about what people want in an educational system. What does it take to create a strong, reliable system that will promote learning, respect, and social responsibility? What I've seen in Finland is a system that sets up quality time on task. The pupils go to school for four and a half hours as first and second graders and then about five and a half hours daily from third through sixth grade. This phenomenon of going to school for a half day and getting excellent results from the pupils is hard for most countries to wrap their heads around. The Finns have not caught the GERM,[1] and they have worked hard to build up an immunity to it by continuing to allow access to physical activity, character development, and curriculum flexibility. The United States has changed dramatically in the wrong direction of what a school day looks like since the 1960s.

As Peter Gray[2] has emphasized, we used to go to school for six hours a day, but for six weeks less per year. Each day had two hours of physical activity: an hour of recess and an hour of physical education. Today, school is conducted, on average, seven and a half hours daily with very little physical activity time included.

In the short term, educators might think children will advance this way, but as we are seeing more and more, children just become much more burned out, stressed out, and physically unhealthy. Force-feeding cognitive information into a child at younger and younger ages in order to pass standardized tests during the school years while discounting the importance of a child's emotional, social, and physical developmental needs creates an unstable environment. This is the mentality that the United States has built themselves around for decades: working longer hours, going to school longer, and practicing a sport more will gain better results. America has all three symptoms of the virus (GERM).

Finland has shown its immunity to the GERM through the following steps. Not only are the pupils going to school for less hours daily, but the amount of time they spend on math, science, Finnish, and history is only a couple hours a day with the seven- and eight-year-olds and approximately three and a half to four hours a day with the nine- to twelve-year-olds. The rest of the day is comprised of physical activity, recess, music, arts and crafts, creative time, and lunch.

In the United States, we pride ourselves on working longer hours to get more done. Do we really get more done? Could we get the same amount of work done in less hours if we focused on the task, then took a break, and repeated that plan throughout the day? What if we left work at a reasonable time and relaxed at home or spent time with family? The GERM has been in the working community for some time, but this high work ethic mentality has now translated to the U.S. schools and sport communities as well. Finnish children rarely take assignments home with them, and they focus on learning content at school for less time with breaks in between, with the end result being better test scores, more productive learning across the students, higher graduation rates, and a stronger middle class.

Parents, administrators, and communities understand how sick our schools and communities are. They are crying out for change in the schools. We all know that more assessments, more time at a desk, and less active time are not the key, but what are we doing? We're applying more assessments and spending more time in the desk and less time being active. This equation continues to produce poorer results!

We need to think about our end goal. If we want quality education, then we need to coordinate our time on task to be focused for shorter periods of time and then take a break. Quantity defined as more hours in schools, more minutes on content daily, and more classroom time is not the answer.

There's another way of putting this: Coaches for many years thought that keeping athletes on the practice field or in the gym for longer hours would produce better performance. What we now know is that less time on the field or in the gym but more focused practice produces better performance. This is the same mind-set I want to see for the U.S. schools. More quality time at the desk means more productive performance based on more focused learning.

So I'll end with the question I began with: What does it take to create a strong, reliable system that will promote learning, respect, and social responsibility? This is not an easy question, but we need to step back and reflect on John Dewey and other developmental psychologists who have paved the way for us. We know what the GERM symptoms are. It's time to eliminate the symptoms by substituting healthy policies, procedures, and practices back into the schools.

REFLECTION 26

AN ADVOCATE FOR CHANGE

Important educational changes are needed in the United States if the learning disparity among children is to decline. It was clear to me when I left Finland that four things are needed in order to right the wrongs we have embraced. One of the individuals who helped to create the success Finland has today is Dr. Pasi Sahlberg. He was the director general of CIMO (National Center for International Mobility and Cooperation) when I visited Finland. This position afforded him the ability to promote internationalization as well as tolerance, creativity, and global ethics in the Finnish society through mobility and institutional cooperation in education, culture, youth, and sport. He not only promoted educational changes in Finland, but also across the globe. He has written several books about the Finnish education system, starting with *Finnish Lessons*,[1] which was instrumental in changing the way people think about education globally.

In order to begin the dialog for systemic change in schools, there was no one better to help shift our thinking than Dr. Sahlberg. I had support from TCU and the Kinesiology Department to have him visit as our kinesiology green chair lecturer to do three days of training with principals, teachers, and superintendents from all across Texas. I asked him to address the four topics that I believe are pivotal to right the wrongs in our educational system: ethics/character, restructuring the school day, more physical education and recess per day, and removal of standardized tests.

Ethics/Character

Ethics is defined as the rules of human conduct with respect to the rightness and wrongness of certain actions and to the goodness and badness of the motives and ends of such actions. Character is defined as the inherent complex of attributes that determines a person's moral and ethical actions and reactions. The educational community has adopted the term *social and emotional learning (SEL)*. It is defined as a process that helps children cultivate essential life skills, including creating awareness of one's own emotions, fostering respect and care for others, establishing strong relationships, making ethical and responsible decisions, and handling adversity constructively.[2]

All of these terms have the same goal, to develop a stronger sense of what is appropriate in the skills mentioned above. Schools must teach the topics in a way that reaches our kids in a fair and unbiased way. Teaching our children about these issues early on and continuing throughout their adolescent years should create a much more responsible adult who makes much wiser choices based on empathy rather than sporadic, selfish choices. Dr. Sahlberg addressed the need for character building in all children and why how we approach this topic is so important.

Restructuring the School Day

American education policy makers have continued over the past decades to increase the amount of time children attend school as well as extending school to younger children. We have gone from a six-hour day to a seven and a half-hour day and from a six-year-old attending school (first grade) to a four-year-old attending school (pre-K). The goal of school should always be driven by developmental principles.

Children ages three to five should not be attending a traditional school setting all day. These children should be playing, exploring, and socializing in an unstructured environment. Dr. Sahlberg discussed why Finland approaches the school day the way they do and how the United States could use similar approaches.

Physical Education/Recess in the Schools

The Finns structure their elementary day around 45 minute content lessons followed by fifteen-minute unstructured, outdoor breaks throughout the day, whereas the United States structures their day around 60 to 120 minute blocks of time in the classroom before changing to a different classroom or having one recess. We treat recess as a one-time event per school day, if that, and think that one 15 to 30 minute break is all children need. The Finns also believe that physical education is just as important as other content areas. Many states do not have physical education requirements in the schools; therefore, recess and physical education become one and the same.

Both structured and unstructured physical activity elements are important to the development of the whole child. Adults forget what it's like to sit in a chair for hours on end before getting to move around again. We forget that children will learn more when allowed to have more outdoor physical activity breaks. We have become so fixated on being better on tests that we have compromised the essential part of our beings, unstructured play and motor skill/manipulative skill development. The inability to move and play has compromised our metabolism and brain function. Dr. Sahlberg addressed the need for unstructured, outdoor play and physical education during the school day.

Removal of Standardized Tests

The United States is infected with the GERM because of standardized tests. The Finns believe that children should have the flexibility to learn without the pressure of standardized testing. Developmental evaluations are much more important to the Finns than standardized tests. They do not grade the children at all until the completion of the fifth grade. Until then, they send home a formal developmental evaluation for each child at the end of each fall and spring semester. Their semesters are equal to ours. They have the same summer breaks and similar holidays throughout the year as we do. Dr. Sahlberg addressed assessments and what we should do differently if we're going to be successful in the United States.

As a result of this three-day workshop, some of the superintendents and principals of schools began to listen. Some of these individuals were looking for a way to bring concepts like these into their schools. As dialog continued, the openness to change became more likely.

EPILOGUE: CREATING A MIND-SET SHIFT IN THE UNITED STATES

So this book is a journey that started in Finland and has grown into my understanding of a culture shift that needs to take place in American schools and most likely in other country's schools as well if a child is going to be whole and healthy and a teacher is going to have the right classroom environment for learning to take place.

The elements I do believe we can adapt from the Finns are the following:

- Standardized assessments must be re-evaluated, and a different assessment system should be utilized to show the strengths of our children instead of their faults.
- Unstructured outdoor play must be the right of the child and offered multiple times daily within the school day.
- Character development should be learned through daily lessons, not philosophy alone.

These types of changes in schools will not be easy. The United States is very committed to a quantity approach for learning and believes the only way children can be successful is to be in an elementary school mind-set from the age of three or four onward. Assessment has become very commonplace, and competition for the best schools is the determinant for a quality education. The GERM is alive and well in America.

Americans are not patient with change. We always want it yesterday. Schools did not get here overnight. A culture shift is needed to make the right moves from our wrong turns. Change takes time and positive energy, just as it did in Finland. Early childhood schools can be positive, but not if the students receive more desk time and less play, exploration, and social time. All schools must include opportunities for children to engage in physical activity, unstructured play, art, music, and crafts. It must also include character skill development.

I am a firm believer in what the public school system can do for American children. I am a product of public schools and want the public schools to again be the strong system they once were. Finland has been able to build and maintain a public school education that is strong and vibrant.

As a result, private schools have not become a necessity there as they have become in the United States. I am an advocate for quality change, and the time is now to create change in our schools focused on quality policies and procedures conducive for the developmental needs of students.

NOTES

Introduction

1 LynNell Hancock, "Why Are Finland's Schools Successful? The Country's Achievements in Education Have Other Nations Doing Their Homework," *The Smithsonian* (September 2011), https://www.smithsonianmag.com/innovation/why-are-finlands-schools-successful-49859555.

2 Centers for Disease Control and Prevention, *The Association between School Based Physical Activity, Including Physical Education, and Academic Performance*, 2010.

3 Dan Rather, "Finnish First," http://www.youtube.com/watch?v=xvBYJBTKRn4&feature=plcp.

4 Amika Singh et al., "Physical Activity and Performance at School: A Systematic Review of the Literature Including a Methodological Quality Assessment," *Archives of Pediatrics & Adolescent Medicine* 166 (2012): 81–99.

5 Francois Trudeau and Roy Shephard, "Relationships of Physical Activity to Brain Health and the Academic Performance of Schoolchildren," *American Journal of Lifestyle Medicine* 4, no. 2 (2010): 138–150.

Crossroads for the United States

1 Cathy Ramstetter and Robert Murray, "Time to Play: Recognizing the Benefits of Recess," *American Educator* (Spring 2017): 17–23.

2 Deborah Rhea, Alexander Rivchun, and Jacqueline Pennings, "The LiiNK Project: Implementation of a Recess and Character Development Pilot Study with Grades K & 1 Children," *Texas Association of Health, Physical Education, Recreation, & Dance Journal* 84, no. 2 (2016): 14–17, 35.

3   "Childhood Obesity: The Challenge," accessed August 2013, http://www.rwjf.org/en/about-rwjf/program-areas/childhood-obesity/the-challenge.html.

4   Centers for Disease Control and Prevention, *School Health Policies and Practices Study: 2014 Overview*, 2015.

5   Erin Howie and Russell Pate, "Physical Activity and Academic Achievement in Children: A Historical Perspective," *Journal of Sport and Health Science* 1 (2012): 160–169.

6   Anthony Pellegrini and Catherine Bohn-Gettler, "The Benefits of Recess in Primary School," *Scholarpedia* 8, no. 2 (2013): 30448.

7   Lindsey Turner, Jamie Chriqui, and Frank Chaloupka, "Withholding Recess from Elementary School Students: Policies Matter," *Journal of School Health* 83 (2013): 533–541.

8   Kathleen Case, Adriana Pérez, Debra Saxton, Deanna Hoelscher, and Andrew Springer, "Bullied Status and Physical Activity in Texas Adolescents," *Health Education & Behavior* 43, no. 3 (2016): 313–320.

9   Bradley Stein and Tamara Dubowitz, "R_x Exercise: Physical Activity Is Good Medicine," *Journal of the American Academy of Child & Adolescent Psychiatry* 54, no. 10 (2015): 795–796.

Reflection 3: The Finnish Student and Pupil – Fitness and Assessment Debate

1   Sharon Plowman and Marilu Meredith (eds.), *Fitnessgram/Activitygram Reference Guide*, 4th ed., http://www.cooperinstitute.org/fitnessgram.

Reflection 5: The Finnish Lifestyle

1   Centers for Disease Control and Prevention, *Comprehensive School Physical Activity Programs: A Guide for Schools*, 2013.

2   United States Department of Health and Human Services (USDHHS), *Physical Activity Guidelines for Americans*, vii, www.health.gov/paguidelines.

3   World Health Organization (WHO), "Physical activity," http://www.who.int/topics/physical_activity/en.

Reflection 9: Perinteissä (Tradition), Perheissä (Family), Sivistys (Culture or Education)

1 "Official Site of the North Pole," https://lapland.nordicvisitor.com/travel-guide/attractions/santa-claus-village.
2 "Official Post Office Site," https://my.posti.fi/en/santa-claus-main-post-office.
3 "Finland Culture Statistics," https://www.commisceo-global.com/resources/country-guides/finland-guide.
4 "Finland Population Statistics," http://www.stat.fi/til/vamuu/2018/08/vamuu_2018_08_2018-09-25_tie_001_en.html.
5 "Finland Sauna Statistics," Stat.fi (in Finnish).
6 Statistics Finland, http://www.stat.fi/til/vamuu/2018/08/vamuu_2018_08_2018-09-25_tie_001_en.html.

Reflection 12: Equity and Excellence

1 Council for the Accreditation of Educator Preparation (CAEP), www.caepnet.org.

Reflection 14: Let's Not Forget the Educational Strengths of the United States

1 John Dewey, *How We Think* (New York: Health, 1933), 85–90.

Reflection 16: Sports, Physical Activity, and Culture—The Vision

1 Finnish Schools on the Move, "Towards More Active and Pleasant School Days," https://liikkuvakoulu.fi/english#haku.
2 Many YouTube videos can be found online showing diabolo demonstrations. The definition of diabolo can be found at https://en.wikipedia.org/wiki/Diabolo.

Reflection 17: Jyväskylä—Where Certified PE Happens

1   Kasper Mäkelä et al., "Job Satisfaction among Physical Education Teachers," *Liikunta & Tiede* 49, no. 1 (2012): 67–74.

Reflection 18: The GERM

1   Pasi Sahlberg, *Finnish Lessons: What Can the World Learn from Educational Change in Finland?* (New York: Teachers College Press, 2011), 1–167.
2   Pasi Sahlberg, GERM, www.pasisahlberg.com/blog.
3   Organization for Economic Co-operation and Development (OECD), http://www.oecd.org/pisa/pisa-2015-results-in-focus.pdf.
4   Center for Public Education, www.centerforpubliceducation.org/research.

Reflection 22: Santa Sighting at the North Pole

1   This website was used for the North Pole history of Rovaniemi, www.santaclausvillage.info.

Reflection 23: The Finnish National Agency for Education

1   Finnish National Agency for Education, "Education System," http://www.oph.fi/english/curricula_and_qualifications.
2   "United States General Population Facts," https://en.wikipedia.org/wiki/United_States.
3   National Center for Educational Statistics, "Public High School Graduation Rates," https://nces.ed.gov/programs/coe/indicator_coi.asp.
4   Michael Cohen, "The State of American High School Graduates: What States Know and Don't Know about Student Performance," *Achieve* (February 2017): 1–43, https://www.achieve.org/files/ACH50CROSS-STATE3.20.17.pdf.

Reflection 25: Quality vs. Quantity (The GERM Mind-set)

1   Pasi Sahlberg, GERM, www.pasisahlberg.com/blog/.
2   Peter Gray, *Free to Learn: Why Unleashing the Instinct to Play Will Make Our Children Happier, More Self-Reliant, and Better Students for Life* (Philadelphia: Basic Books, 2013).

Reflection 26: An Advocate for Change

1   Pasi Sahlberg, *Finnish Lessons: What Can the World Learn from Educational Change in Finland?* (New York: Teachers College Press, 2011), 1–167.
2   Nadja Reilly, "The Bonds of Social-Emotional Learning," *Mental Health in Schools* 75 (2017): 56–60.

BIBLIOGRAPHY

Case, Kathleen, Adriana Pérez, Debra Saxton, Deanna Hoelscher, and Andrew Springer. "Bullied Status and Physical Activity in Texas Adolescents." *Health Education & Behavior* 43, no. 3 (2016): 313–320.

Centers for Disease Control and Prevention. *School Health Policies and Practices Study: 2014 Overview*. Atlanta: US Department of Health and Human Services, 2015.

———. *Comprehensive School Physical Activity Programs: A Guide for Schools*. Atlanta: U.S. Department of Health and Human Services, 2013.

———. *The Association between School Based Physical Activity, Including Physical Education, and Academic Performance*. Atlanta: U.S. Department of Health and Human Services, 2010.

Center for Public Education. www.centerforpubliceducation.org/research.

"Childhood Obesity: The Challenge." Robert Wood Johnson Foundation. Accessed August 2013. http://www.rwjf.org/en/about-rwjf/program-areas/childhood-obesity/the-challenge.html.

Cohen, Michael. "The State of American High School Graduates: What States Know and Don't Know about Student Performance." *Achieve* (February 2017): 1–43. https://www.achieve.org/files/ACH50CROSS-STATE3.20.17.pdf

Dan Rather's Report. "Finnish First." HDNet, aired on April 3, 2012. Excerpt: http://www.youtube.com/watch?v=xvBYJBTKRn4&feature=plcp.

Dewey, John. *How We Think*. New York: Health, 1933.

Finnish National Agency for Education. "Education System." (2018). http://www.oph.fi/english/curricula_and_qualifications.

Finnish Schools on the Move. "Towards More Active and Pleasant School Days." *2015–2016 Report*. https://liikkuvakoulu.fi/english#haku.

Gray, Peter. *Free to Learn: Why Unleashing the Instinct to Play Will Make Our Children Happier, More Self-Reliant, and Better Students for Life*. Philadelphia: Basic Books, 2013.

Hancock, LynNell. "Why Are Finland's Schools Successful? The Country's Achievements in Education Have Other Nations Doing Their Homework." *The Smithsonian* (September 2011). https://www.smithsonianmag.com/innovation/why-are-finlands-schools-successful-49859555.

Howie, Erin, and Russell Pate. "Physical Activity and Academic Achievement in Children: A Historical Perspective." *Journal of Sport and Health Science* 1 (2012): 160–169.

Institute of Education Sciences (IES). National Center for Educational Statistics. 2016. https://nces.ed.gov/programs/coe/indicator_coi.asp.

Mäkelä, Kasper, Mirja Hirvensalo, Sanna Palomäki, Heikki Herva, and Lauri Laakso. "Job Satisfaction Among Physical Education Teachers." *Liikunta & Tiede* 49, no. 1 (2012): 67–74.

Organization for Economic Co-operation and Development (OECD). PISA 2015 Results in Focus. (2016). http://www.oecd.org/pisa/pisa-2015-results-in-focus.pdf.

Pellegrini, Anthony, and Catherine Bohn-Gettler. "The Benefits of Recess in Primary School." *Scholarpedia* 8, no. 2 (2013): 30448.

Plowman, Sharon, and Marilu Meredith, eds. *Fitnessgram/ Activitygram Reference Guide*, 4th ed. Dallas: The Cooper Institute, 2013. http://www.cooperinstitute.org/fitnessgram.

Ramstetter, Cathy, and Robert Murray. "Time to Play: Recognizing the Benefits of Recess." *American Educator* (Spring 2017): 17–23.

Reilly, Nadja. "The Bonds of Social-Emotional Learning." *Mental Health in Schools* 75, (2017): 56–60.

Rhea, Deborah, Alexander Rivchun, and Jacqueline Pennings. "The LiiNK Project: Implementation of a Recess and Character Development Pilot Study with Grades K & 1 Children." *Texas Association of Health, Physical Education, Recreation, & Dance Journal* 84, no. 2 (2016): 14–17, 35.

Sahlberg, Pasi. *Finnish Lessons: What Can the World Learn from Educational Change in Finland?* New York: Teachers College Press, 2011.

———. GERM. 2013. www.pasisahlberg.com/blog.

Singh, Amika, Leonie Uijtdewilligen, Jos Twisk, Willem van Mechelen, and Mai Chinapaw. "Physical Activity and Performance at School: A Systematic Review of the Literature Including a Methodological Quality Assessment." *Archives of Pediatrics & Adolescent Medicine* 166 (2012): 81–99.

Stein, Bradley, and Tamara Dubowitz. "R_x Exercise: Physical Activity Is Good Medicine." *Journal of the American Academy of Child & Adolescent Psychiatry* 54, no. 10 (2015): 795–796.

Trudeau, Francois, and Roy Shephard. "Relationships of Physical Activity to Brain Health and the Academic Performance of Schoolchildren." *American Journal of Lifestyle Medicine*, 4, no. 2 (2010): 138–150.

Turner, Lindsey, Jamie Chriqui, and Frank Chaloupka. "Withholding Recess from Elementary School Students: Policies Matter." *Journal of School Health* 83 (2013): 533–541.

United States Department of Health and Human Services (USDHHS). *Physical Activity Guidelines for Americans.* Washington, DC: 2008. www.health.gov/paguidelines.

World Health Organization (WHO). "Physical Activity." http://www.who.int/topics/physical_activity/en.

APPENDIX A

Finland Six-Week Schedule

Week 37

Monday   Arrived in Helsinki; checked into apartment; emailed my three assigned sponsors from University of Helsinki (will call them Faculty 1, 2, and 3)

Tuesday   10:00–11:00—met with University of Helsinki sponsors

11:30–1:00—had lunch with faculty sponsors

1:00–3:00—discussed schedule for the next two weeks and received office keys where I would share desk space with Faculty 1

Wednesday 8:00–10:00—observed Faculty 2 in an assessment and evaluation class he teaches

10:00–11:00—had meeting with Faculty 1 and 3

11:00–1:00—observed a track and field methods class with Faculty 2

2:00–4:00—debriefed with Faculty 2 after the observation

Thursday   11:00–2:00—had lunch with Faculty 3

2:00–4:00—observed lesson Faculty 3 taught for adventure education

Friday   8:00–4:00—met Faculty 1 and her class at Lake Kuusijärvi to observe and participate in outdoor education (methods class for this cohort of majors). Warm clothes were needed this day. We had a cookout after morning activities.

Week 38

Monday   8:00–9:00—walked to university office

9:00–10:00—met with Faculty 1 before class

10:00–12:00—attended PE, society, and health lecture

2:00–4:00—met with Faculty 1 to go over events from today

Tuesday   8:30–10:00—met with dean of college

10:00–12:00—met with chair of department

1:00–4:00—observed methods class with Faculty 2 regarding Finnish baseball techniques

Wednesday   8:00–3:00—observed in elementary school setting (including grades one through three classrooms) physical education and recess several times and interviewed a principal

Thursday   8:00–3:00—observed in elementary/middle school setting (including grades four through eight) classrooms, physical education, music, art, and crafts

Friday   8:00–3:00—observed Faculty 2's methods class working with grades three through eight school students on outdoor education

Week 39

Monday	8:30–12:00—observed elementary school (grades one through six)
Tuesday	8:00–1:00—took a bus to observe elementary school teachers
	1:00–3:00—returned to University of Helsinki to meet with dance methods faculty and observe her class
Wednesday	8:00–1:00—took a bus to observe elementary school teachers and first aid observation with teacher and students
	9:45–1:00—observed elementary grades outdoor education with Faculty 3
	2:00–4:00—met with Faculty 1 to go over events from the day.
Thursday	8:00–1:00—travelled to Espoo and observed kindergarten children working on adventure education
	I was instructed to wear warm clothes. It was all outside and very cold, windy, and rainy.
Friday	8:00–9:00—met with Sports Federation representative
	9:00–12:00—observed Faculty 2's methods class students presenting their grand finale projects with grades three through eight school pupils (map reading)
	2:00–4:00—met with Faculty 1 to go over events from the week and travel plans/schedule for Jyväskylä on Sunday

Week 40

Sunday   Left for Jyväskylä by train

              6:00—arrived at Jyväskylä, where university lecturer from College of Education picked me up and took me to hotel

              Dropped off to check in and get ready for the next two days of observations and interviews

Monday   9:00—met professor from Faculty of Sport and Health Sciences, who transported me to the University of Jyväskylä

              10:00–4:00—attended scheduled program with the faculty of Sport and Health Sciences; observed physical education teacher education at the university; had lunch; observed student lessons (master's thesis class, motor learning lecture, and teacher training in aerobic class); observed research and teaching adapted physical education; went to the home of a professor for Finnish food snacks and debriefing

Tuesday   9:00–2:00—attended program at the university with faculty of Sport and Health Sciences

              2:00–5:00—met university lecturer to talk about constructing the future school community

              5:15—left on train departed for Helsinki

Wednesday   8:00–4:00—observed at one of the comprehensive schools (grades one through nine)

Thursday   8:00–3:00—observed at a high school

Friday   8:00–2:00—observed at a high school

Week 41

Monday	9:00–5:00—departed for Espoo and observed in a middle-school setting
Tuesday	9:00–2:00—observed art and music classes at the university
Wednesday	9:00–3:00—visited with religion and philosophy professors about university and public school teachings as well as observed ethics and religion taught in elementary school setting
Thursday	8:00–3:00—observed unstructured play with different grade levels and travelled to indoor swimming pool to watch pupils learn how to swim (grades one through three)
Friday	8:00–2:00—observed at a high school, watched unstructured play breaks with high school pupils, and watched different activities each break time (breaks were longer but fewer of them). Departed for Rovaniemi for the weekend by plane Arrived back Sunday evening

Week 42

Monday	8:00–2:00—observed an international school for all grade levels
Tuesday	9:00–2:00—observed dance classes for grades seven through twelve
Wednesday	9:00–3:00—observed elementary lab school to observe all kinds of content classes and unstructured outdoor play as well as observed transitions, dressing for cold weather to go outside

Thursday	8:00–3:00—observed unstructured play with different grade levels and spent quite a bit of time with Faculty 1 and 2 debriefing and gathering last-minute information
Friday	8:00–2:00—spent most of the day with Faculty 1 and 2 and discussed research for future activities between TCU and University of Helsinki Departed for Fort Worth, Texas

Six-week trip complete

APPENDIX B

Distribution of Content Hours Weekly Grades 1–9

Distribution of lesson hours in basic education

(Government Decree 28.6.2012)

Subjects / Grades	1 2	3 4 5 6	7 8 9	Total
Mother tongue and literature	14	18	10	42
A-1 language	------------	9	7	16
B1-language	--------------------------------2		4	6
Mathematics	6	15	11	32
Environmental studies	4	10		
Biology and geography[1]			7	
Physics and chemistry[1]			7	
Health education[1]			3	
Environment & nature studies in total		*14*	*17*	31
Religion/Ethics	2	5	3	10
History and social studies[2]	------------	------------ 5	7	12
Music	2	4	2	8
Visual arts	2	5	2	9
Crafts	4	5	2	11
Physical education	4	9	7	20
Home economics	------------------------------------		3	3
Artistic & practical elective subjects		6	5	11
Artistic & practical subjects in total				62
Guidance counselling	------------------------------------		2	2
Optional subjects		9		9
Minimum number of lessons				222
(Optional A2-language)[3]	------------	(12)		12
(Optional B2-language)[3]	------------------------------------		(4)	(4)

--- =Subject is taught in the grades if started in the local curriculum.

[1] The subject is taught as a part of the integrated environmental studies in the grades 1-6.

[2] Social studies are taught in grades 4-6 for at least 2 hours per week and grades 7-9 at least 3 hours per week.

[3] The pupil can, depending on the language, study a free-choice A2 language either as an optional subject or instead of the B1 language.

The pupil can study the B2 language as an optional subject. The free-choice A2 and B2 languages can, alternatively, be organized as instruction exceeding the minimum time allocation. In this case their instruction cannot be organized using the minimum time allocated in the distribution of lesson hours for optional or B1 language as defined in this paragraph. Depending on the language the pupil receives instruction in a B1 language or optional subjects instead of this B1 language. The distribution of lesson hours would be a minimum of 234 annual lessons for a pupil studying the A2 language as instruction exceeding the minimum time allocation. The corresponding number of annual lessons is a minimum of 226 for a pupil with the B2 language. The total number of annual lessons would be a minimum of 238 for pupils studying both the A2 and the B1 languages as instruction exceeding the minimum time allocation.

Distribution of Lesson Hours in Basic Education

Printed in the United States
By Bookmasters